WEST UKRAINIAN NATIONAL UNIVERSITY

WEST UKRAINIAN
NATIONAL
UNIVERSITY

55th Anniversary
of WUNU

Volodymyr Muravskyi

ACCOUNTING AND CYBERSECURITY

Monograph

Scientific Editor
Doctor of Economics, Professor
Z.-M. V. Zadorognyi

2021

UDC 657:004
ISBN 978-0-578-33183-6

Reviewers:

Lehenchuk Serhiy Fedorovych, Doctor of Economics, Professor, Head of the Department of Information Systems in Management and Accounting of Zhytomyr Polytechnic State University;

Sadovska Iryna Borysivna, Doctor of Economics, Professor, Head of the Department of Accounting and Taxation of Lesya Ukrainka Volyn National University;

Shyhun Maria Mykhailivna, Doctor of Economics, Professor, Head of the Department of Accounting and Consulting, Kyiv National Economic University named after Vadym Hetman.

Under scientific editorial supervision of Doctor of Economics,
Professor Z.-M. V. Zadorozhnyi

Recommended for publication by the decision of the Academic Council of West Ukrainian National University (Protocol № 3, November 16, 2021)

Muravskyi, Volodymyr. Accounting and Cybersecurity: Monograph. Scientific Editor – Z.-M. V. Zadorozhnyi. Kindle Publishing, Seattle. USA. 2021. 200 p.

ISBN 978-0-578-33183-6

The monograph examines the theoretical and applied aspects of the development of accounting to ensure cybersecurity of enterprises. The positioning of the accounting system as a platform for the organization of economic and information security of enterprises is proposed. The classification of cyber risks in accounting and users of accounting information is improved to prevent and eliminate cyber threats. A method of accounting for individual accounting objects using information and communication technologies to ensure cybersecurity of enterprises is developed. The organizational features of accounting in the context of the organization of cybersecurity of enterprises are considered.

The monograph will be useful for accounting professionals, scientists, teachers, graduate students, doctoral students, students of economic and technical specialties and anyone interested in the problems of computerization of accounting, control, management.

INDEX

PREFACE

Emergence of the digital economy, the growing number of global hybrid conflicts, social distancing and remote operation of enterprises in a pandemic has led to an increase in cyber threats to economic systems at micro and macro levels. The active development of computer and communication technologies in the digital economy has led to a variety of cyber threats aimed at providing third parties with economic benefits or causing enterprises economic damages due to the expansion of facilities and vulnerabilities in information system of enterprises. Since accounting is the main generator of economic information, accounting information requires foremost cybersecurity. Ensuring cybersecurity involves not only protecting accounting data, but also making accounting the actor in the security processes. It is necessary to involve accounting specialists in the issues of enterprise cybersecurity.

Cybersecurity of enterprises, sectors and industries entails information protection and prevention of organisational, technological, PR and investment losses using accounting techniques. Regardless of the type of cyberattack, it is important to focus on universal principles of prevention, avoidance and elimination of the consequences of threats to the security of accounting information. Ensuring effective cybersecurity of enterprises requires improvement of the theory, methodology, applied and organization of accounting.

Therefore the monograph consists of three chapters: "Theoretical foundations of the relationship between accounting and cybersecurity of enterprises", "Improving accounting methods for the purposes of cybersecurity of enterprises", "Organization of accounting to ensure cyber protection of enterprises". The monograph is intended to be used by researchers, lecturers, teachers, doctoral and post-graduate students of economic and technical specialties specialties of higher education institutions as well as for managers, accountants, economists and cybersecurity professionals at the enterprises.

CHAPTER 1. THEORETICAL FOUNDATIONS OF THE RELATIONSHIP BETWEEN ACCOUNTING AND CYBERSECURITY OF ENTERPRISES

1.1. The accounting system as the basis for organising enterprise cybersecurity

Ensuring the cybersecurity of economic systems is an important element of protection against the hybrid influence on state and non-state institutions. Cybersecurity of enterprises, sectors and industries entails information protection and prevention of organisational, technological, PR and investment losses. Given that the accounting system generates economic information, it is necessary to involve accounting specialists in the issues of enterprise cybersecurity. The accounting system as one of the enterprise management functions is a primary source of the information processes, therefore it takes priority in cyber protection.

At first, the need for ensuring cybersecurity was viewed as merely an element of information cycle of the enterprise in order to prevent losses in consumer value of accounting data, third parties accessing accounting data, or unauthorised employee use of information resources, etc. This purely informational approach to cybersecurity is partial and does not allow for the systematic provision of cybersecurity for businesses, industries or national economic systems.

The catalyst for comprehensive scientific applied research on the security of accounting data was the repeated cyber threat of international scope in the course of the hybrid wars. The scale and global nature of the cybersecurity issue determine the need to ensure the informational and economic security of countries. The European countries like Britain, France, Lithuania, Estonia and Spain have the highest level of cybersecurity (Global Cybersecurity Index, 2019) (Tabl. 1.1).

Table 1.1

European countries ranked by Cybersecurity Index

Country	Score	Regional Rank 2018	Global Rank 2018	Global Rank 2017	Dif. 2018/2017
United Kingdom	0.931	1	1	12	+11
France	0.918	2	3	8	+5
Lithuania	0.908	3	4	56	+52
Estonia	0.905	4	5	5	+0
Spain	0.896	5	7	19	+12
Norway	0.892	6	9	11	+2
Luxembourg	0.886	7	11	36	+25
Netherlands	0.885	8	12	15	+3
Georgia	0.857	9	18	8	-10
Finland	0.856	10	19	16	-3
Turkey	0.853	11	20	43	+23
Denmark	0.852	12	21	34	+13
Germany	0.849	13	22	24	+2
Croatia	0.840	14	24	41	+17
Italy	0.837	15	25	31	+6
Austria	0.826	16	28	30	+2
Poland	0.815	17	29	33	+4
Belgium	0.814	18	30	27	-3
Hungary	0.812	19	31	51	+20
Sweden	0.810	20	32	17	-15
North Macedonia	0.800	21	34	54	+20
Switzerland	0.788	22	37	18	-19
Ireland	0.784	23	38	26	-12
Israel	0.783	24	39	20	-19
Portugal	0.758	25	42	55	+13
Monaco	0.751	26	43	102	+59
Latvia	0.748	27	44	21	-23
Slovakia	0.729	28	45	81	+36
Bulgaria	0.721	29	46	44	-2
Slovenia	0.701	30	48	83	+35
Moldova	0.662	31	53	72	+19
Ukraine	0.661	32	54	58	+4
Cyprus	0.652	33	56	60	+4
Serbia	0.643	34	58	89	+31
Montenegro	0.639	35	61	70	+9
Albania	0.631	36	62	88	+26
Czech Republic	0.569	37	71	35	-36
Romania	0.568	38	72	42	-30
Liechtenstein	0.543	39	75	111	+36
Greece	0.527	40	77	63	-14

Source: compiled by the author on the basis (Global Cybersecurity Index, 2019)

Due to the increased cyber influence that national information environments have been subjected to in the recent years, most European countries have made efforts to better their global cybersecurity ratings. In particular, Lithuania climbed 36 places in the rating, Serbia – 31, Slovenia – 35, Slovakia – 52.

Ukraine's advance in the global cybersecurity rating is explained by the increased attention to data protection at the micro-level. Most big businesses of national importance have opened vacancies or entire departments for employees whose operational responsibilities include ensuring cybersecurity. However, gradually all enterprises regardless of size or scope experienced the need to ensure the cybersecurity of economic operations because of the frequent hacks, commercial secrets theft, virus modules embedded in software allowing benefit through fraudulent means and so on.

Many scientists have researched the problems of accounting data security in conditions of active cyber threats at micro and macro levels. In particular, Yu. Moroz and Yu. Tsal-Tsalko formulated a comprehensive definition of "cybersecurity" from the accounting point of view. They define it as the security from internal and external threats of the enterprise's vital interests, human and intellectual capital, trade secrets, proprietary technologies, profits, added and market value, information created by the accounting system and provided for by special legal, economic, organisational, informational and technical measures (Moroz and Tsal-Tsalko, 2017). S. Viter and I. Svitlyshyn determined the fundamental principles of measures for accounting data cybersecurity, namely: software support, protection of confidential information, personal responsibility, confidentiality, comprehensiveness, and control over access to accounting data (Viter and Svitlyshyn, 2017).

Most scientists attribute the need for cybersecurity at micro and macro levels to the increasing development of computer and communication technologies. Due to the digitalisation of socio-economic processes and the emergence of cyberspace, there have been more and more criminal acts aimed at causing harm and illegal financial gain. The need for more active cybersecurity as a result of increased level of information processing technologies in social and economic activities has been disproven by the latest global research (Global Cybersecurity Index, 2019).

The analysis of the relationship between ICT development and the level of cybersecurity allows us to conclude that there is an imbalance between these indicators in many countries. In other words, there is no direct dependence of the development of cybersecurity systems on the level of digitisation of socio-economic processes in the country. The frequency and types of cyber threats thus are given priority when justifying the urgency of bolstering the cybersecurity of a country. Therefore, the main factor driving the improvement of cybersecurity is not the level of digitisation of socio-economic activities, but rather the likelihood of information barriers and risks.

This position is properly argued in the research of Diane Janvrin and Tawei Wang who have traced the chronology of the concept "cybersecurity" and its development in accounting terms. The scientists have concluded that 2019, considering the high number of cyberattacks, was the turning point in the development of research on the security of accounting systems at enterprises (Janvrin and Wang, 2019). Elina Haapamäki and Jukka Sihvonen have confirmed that the research on accounting elements of cybersecurity of enterprises has intensified. They have noted a growing number of scientific papers dedicated to the security topics in 2008-2020, which is proportional to the number of cyberattacks (Haapamäki and Sihvonen, 2019).

Nevertheless, the identification and classification of measures combatting information barriers and threats to the operation of the enterprise's accounting system remains the most discussed issue. For example, V. Shpak distinguishes four groups of such measures: legal, technical, software and organisational (Shpak, 2015). S. Denha and Y.

Veryha differentiate active and passive methods of minimising threats to accounting information systems. Active methods include prevention of computer fraud and sabotage, passive – reduction of errors by accounting specialists and breakdowns of accounting software and hardware (Denha and Veryha, 2004). I. Hrabchuk proposes methods of logical (ensuring informational security of the enterprise as a part of corporate culture) and physical security (data encryption and physical protection of hardware) (Hrabchuk, 2018).

However, scientific and applied research that is more systemic is required to understand the economic aspect of information security. It entails determining the relationship between the types of cyber threats and methods of combatting them. In particular, Tim Eaton, Jonathan Grenier, and David Layman have substantiated the need for a correlation study on information barriers classification in accounting and the specific methods of risk management at the enterprise (Eaton et al., 2019). Yu. Popivniak has also distinguished between organisational, personnel, technological and legal cyber threats and corresponding ways of eliminating them in the conditions of using new information technologies such as blockchain, cloud storage, etc. (Popivniak, 2019). The influence of blockchain technology on cybersecurity of the accounting system has been researched by Sebahattin Demirkan, Irem Demirkan and Andrew Mckee. Using the accounting system in the USA, the scientists predicted an increase of Big Data sets and substantiated the importance of structuring and managing them with blockchain technology in order to ensure information security (Demirkan et al., 2020).

Framework of operational responsibilities of accounting personnel in the event of cyberattacks is an important direction of research that establishes the role of accounting in ensuring security. For instance, Laura Schaffner Georg et al. have developed instructions for avoiding, overcoming and minimising the effects of the cyber impact on economic systems of the enterprise (Schaffner, 2018). Similarly, V. Rozheliuk has outlined the measures aimed at minimising internal, accidental and external threats to cybersecurity. Whilst doing so, she defined cybersecurity of the enterprise as a set of actions carried out by accounting personnel with the purpose of archiving data, maintaining the professionalism level of accounting specialists, building an effective communication system between the enterprise and the stakeholders, creating optimal work conditions for accountants, and so on (Rozheliuk, 2013).

John Pendley has justified the involvement of accounting specialists in the development of information technologies (software and hardware) dealing with cybersecurity. According to the scientist, effective operation of the cybersecurity system for economic processes is impossible without the participation of accounting and control specialists (Pendley,). Some researchers have concluded that tech specialists (system administrators, programmers, corporate architects, database administrators, etc.) are incapable of ensuring the system cybersecurity that emphasises the optimisation of economic operations at enterprises. Thomas Heaton Spitters has published a booklet dedicated solely to instructing accountants on how to act in the event of cyber threats. The scientific paper is one of the first attempts of systematically analyse the accounting aspect of security processes (Spitters, 2019).

Most scientific papers treat the accounting system as the object protected by the cybersecurity of the enterprise. This approach is scientifically limited, as it does not consider that the accounting system may be the subject ensuring the cybersecurity of enterprises in the conditions of rapid development of latest computer and communication technologies. It is recommended to associate the cybersecurity functions with the accounting system of the enterprise in order to optimize the information and security processes.

Ensuring cybersecurity involves not only protecting accounting data, but also making accounting the actor in the security processes. A hypothesis of scientific and applied research is proposed, according to which accounting is the basis for ensuring cybersecurity of enterprises and the integrator of methodological and organisational actions aimed at maintaining information and economic security of economic entities, branches and sectors of the economy.

The proposed hypothesis on viewing the accounting system as a platform for organising cybersecurity is supported by the empirical experience of enterprises that practise information security measures.

The underlying rationale for the scientific hypothesis determines that:

- the accounting system is the main producer of economic information, therefore the accounting processes should be prioritised in cybersecurity matters;
- much of the accounting information (excluding the data produced by financial accounting) contains trade secrets as it is used for the operational, tactical and strategic planning by the management;
- the latest hacker attacks and fraudulent schemes have been conducted through accounting and management software (Pety.A virus in the M.E.Doc program, power outages because of hacker attacks), which explains the importance of protecting the accounting system;
- modern accountants are multi-qualified professionals who combine economic, technical and legal knowledge and can perform cybersecurity functions at the enterprise;
- the regulatory framework for the accounting system defines most information processes at the enterprise and some regulations may contain guidelines on ensuring cybersecurity.

Expounding on the aforementioned hypothesis of developing the methodology and framework of accounting geared towards maintaining cybersecurity of the enterprise requires a complex of scientific and applied research and development (Fig. 1.1).

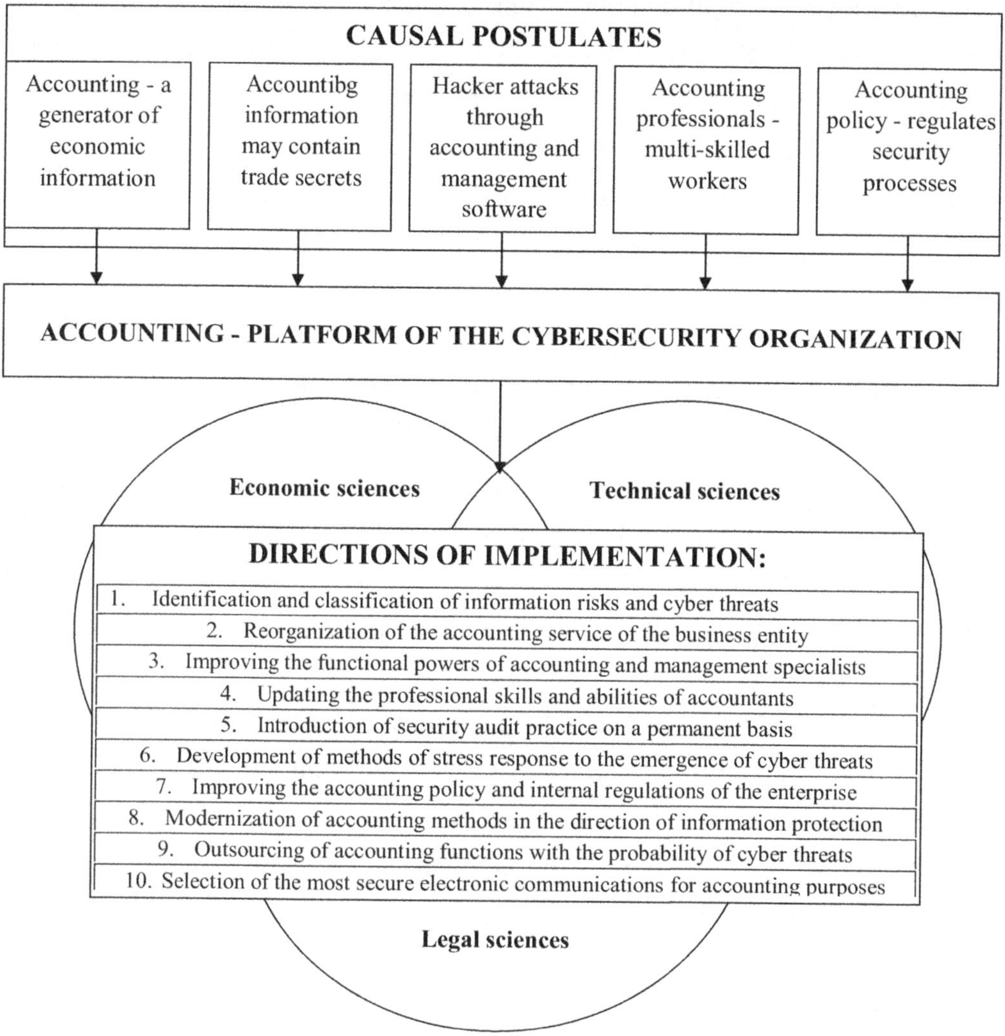

Fig. 1.1. Positioning of accounting as a center of organization of cybersecurity of enterprises

Organization of cybersecurity using the accounting system as the basis entails the expansion of the operational responsibilities of the accounting and internal control departments or an addition of the cybersecurity specialist post to the enterprise's staff. The feasibility of organisational transformations must be justified by their economic effectiveness, regardless of the size and scope of the business. According to the Internet Security Threat Report (2019), 80% of cybercrime targeted small businesses through mail services, social networks, and cloud services in 2019. The main reason cyberattacks centre on small-scale business is the lack of specialists and departments ensuring cybersecurity. Therefore, the likelihood that these cyberattacks will be successful on such businesses is higher. Specialists on accounting or control can successfully perform the cybersecurity functions at small enterprises.

Therefore, cybersecurity specialists should divided into 3 groups: specialists on information security (accounting staff), control department specialists (testing information systems on vulnerability to breaches, cybersecurity analysts, internal controllers, security auditors, inspectors on confidential information security), and technical support staff (system administrators, computer network administrators, programmers of specialised systems and web technology).

It would be prudent to instruct the employees of the first category in the course of the accounting specialists' professional training. The second group may consist of the accounting personnel who have practical experience in the field of cybersecurity and have acquired additional multidisciplinary skills and knowledge. Only the employees of the third group would be trained in the 'tech field' that does not envision obtaining in-depth knowledge of the economic disciplines, including accounting, analysis and control.

Thus, the operational responsibilities of accounting specialists of the first and the second group include: identifying vulnerabilities of the information systems and modelling the likely scenarios of cyber threats and risks related to them; verifying the reliability of security system operation, developing security measures in the event of unforeseen circumstances; classifying accounting information as restricted (commercial and trade secrets, other confidential information); developing regulations, policies and procedures in the framework of accounting information security; implementing developed security measures, testing the system in order to evaluate its effectiveness, and making adjustments as needed; assigning the necessary security details to the accounting computer system users; teaching the rules of continuous information processing to information system users; ensuring that information system users and company staff adhere to the rules of working with accounting information (Viter and Svitlyshyn, 2017).

It is important to regulate the operational responsibilities of cybersecurity in the employee handbook of accounting specialists and to define liability for violations of enterprise cybersecurity. Such responsibility may be not only administrative but also criminal, as the actions of accounting specialists may harm both the cybersecurity of a single enterprise and the national security of an entire sector of the economy.

Additionally it is recommended to recognize the responsibility for effective cybersecurity of the enterprise in the Ethics Code of Professional Accountants. In particular, the meaning of confidentiality – one of the accounting services principles stipulating that accounting information must not be disclosed to third parties – should be expanded to include the definition of the accounting specialist as the organiser of data security. Security privileges should be documented in the employee handbook along with any changes to the accounting policy of the enterprise. The procedure for protecting accounting data must be outlined in the main the regulatory document of accounting – the accounting policy of the enterprise.

Combining all regulations on cybersecurity in the accounting policy will ensure that the enterprise operation goals, its accounting, analytical, control and management systems correspond to effective cybersecurity. Usefulness of any change in an accounting or management can be assessed by the influence it has on the cybersecurity of the enterprise – either strengthening or weakening it. The integrated document (set of documents) on regulating cybersecurity is the main guideline for conducting internal and external security audit. It is recommended to monitor the cybersecurity system continuously in order to evaluate the quality of information security at the enterprise. According to a study by CyberEdge Group, it has been discovered that 78% of cyberattacks on enterprises employing cybersecurity specialists were successful (approximately 63% of all enterprises were subject to such threats) in 2019 (2019 Cyberthreat Defense Report, 2019). In other words, a cybersecurity system is not a guarantee that the enterprise will have comprehensive protection against all threats. The structure of cybersecurity system may have weaknesses the detection of which requires engaging the services of security audit.

Internal accounting specialists may be authorised to conduct continuous security audit, or this function may be outsourced to external independent auditor and consulting firms. The main task of security audit is to provide a comprehensive systemic evaluation of information risks that jeopardise economic processes and the cybersecurity of the enterprise. Cybersecurity specialists must have a comprehensive understanding of information processes at the enterprise, the information and technological infrastructure, the interactions with external stakeholders and contractors, and the algorithm automating management through specialised software, legal aspects of business operations, and so on. All this knowledge is largely accumulated by accounting specialists.

Additionally, accounting specialists, contrary to today, should monitor the effectiveness of firewalls, the latest antivirus software, the update state of specialized computer programs to the latest versions, as well as the use of strong passwords by employees to protect confidential information. A comprehensive combination of these skills and knowledge will allow security auditors to monitor the internal and external threats. An effective method of monitoring the state of cybersecurity is testing the company's information system. A revision of internal and external communication should be conducted, which would create an opportunity for an analysis of information flows being leaked. Creation and use of information containing trade secrets requires continuous monitoring.

The most time consuming part of the security audit is testing the company staff regarding the possible confidential information leaks. Security auditors can make use of the phishing mailing lists in order to identify the enterprise employees who are vulnerable to cyber threats and ready to disclose personal confidential data. Internal auditors must then work further with the identified personnel who may violate information security in order to update their security skills and habits. It is also important to test the specialised software for vulnerability to cyber threats and the ability of antivirus computer programs to detect various types of viruses. The results of software tests may lead to a decision on replacing or upgrading it.

The system of admittance to and protection of facilities and grounds of the enterprise requires further testing. Security auditors can control the restrictions on entering certain areas and internal spaces of economic entities in order to develop recommendations on improving the security service, the guard posts, video surveillance, and biometric identification of staff.

If it is impossible to organise permanent and effective internal security audit, the management of the business entity may turn to external audit firms. Moreover, in 2019 approximately 84% of companies sent their cybersecurity experts for retraining (refreshment course) leading to significant administrative costs, according to the Telstra Security Report (Summary Report / Telstra Security Report 2019, 2019). The enterprise may engage security outsourcing to minimise the costs of training personnel. According to the data of the Chartered Institute of Management Accountants, most British audit firms in England and Wales provide security audit services (Risk committees, 2020). Large audit companies are actively opening vacancies for cybersecurity experts and facilitating the re-training of auditors with an emphasis on ensuring information security of business entities, who are the customers of audit services.

The market for cybersecurity services is growing rapidly. More and more often, audit firms are offering services on setting up the cybersecurity at enterprises in addition to security audit. Independent outsourcers accumulate risks and responsibilities for cyberattacks on businesses. In addition to a professional approach to cybersecurity, security professionals are able to respond quickly to any emerging threats. According to Telstra, 78% of companies did not have a clear response plan to possible threats in 2019 (Summary Report / Telstra Security Report 2019, 2019), and therefore needed to involve external auditors in developing security policy in case of active threats.

Timely response to cyberattacks makes it possible to avoid information and, accordingly, economic and PR losses. Auditors are able to respond independently to certain cyber threats or provide advice to accounting specialists on eliminating them. The efficiency of anti-crisis management largely depends on the model of interaction between the audit firm and the accounting department of the enterprise that requires further scientific research on security issues.

1.2. Principles of cybersecurity of accounting information

In the information society and its economic dimension – digital economy, information is the main subject of work of business entities. Computer and communication technology, the use of which leads to cyber risks, is increasingly used as a means of work. Attackers are interested in information systems of enterprises to cause economic damage or getting gain. Information that contains commercial interest becomes mainly the object of cyber incidents.

The activities of attackers are also focused on distortion of accounting information. Due to submission of partial or incorrect records to stakeholders, it is possible to cause economic damage to both senders and recipients of information. On the basis of incorrect accounting information, ineffective management decisions are made. Similarly, obtaining untimely accounting information or blocking access to information resources leads to delayed management of enterprises.

Taking into account the variability of cyber risks,it is necessary to develop universal principles for prevention, avoiding and eliminating the consequences of threats to the security of accounting information. Regardless of the type of cyberattack, it is important to focus on universal principles of prevention, avoidance and elimination of the consequences of threats to the security of accounting information. The principles are the basis for developing guidelines for cybersecurity of accounting information. The use of standardized rules of cybersecurity of enterprises provides effective and risk-free management of economic entities.

The principles of processing and preparation of accounting information are actively studied by scientists. Most of the authors position the quality of accounting information as a defining characteristic of information resources. However, the necessity for ensuring cybersecurity of enterprises, actualizes a slightly different approach to determining the fundamental field of accounting. In the first place in the study of the principles of preparation of accounting information the reliability as the ability to avoid and eliminate cyber threats are put forward. For example, V.V. Yevdokimov defines the principle of reliability along with availability and feasibility as a prerequisite for ensuring the economic security of enterprises (Yevdokymov, 2011). Reliability as an important characteristic of functioning of information systems is considered by O. Saydjari (2019) in the context of the organization of an effective system of cybersecurity of enterprises. Instead L.O. Kyrylieva and A.O. Postavny (2010) offer the principle of confidential accounting information as a basis for cybersecurity of enterprises, which is a somewhat limited view on cybersecurity.

Mariana Hentea defines the basic conceptual principles of cybersecurity in consisting of: risk, vulnerability, threat, attack, impact, consequences and control (Hentea, 2021). However, such scientific approach makes it possible to identify the conceptual concepts used in the cybersecurity of accounting information, but not the principles. Marc Dupuis and Karen Renaud discuss the ethical principles of cybersecurity related to overcoming the fear of cyber threats (Dupuis and Renaud, 2020). Paul Rosenzweig has developed ten principles of cybersecurity of information, which are mainly related to the active development of Internet technologies (Rosenzweig, 2011). However, the given principles are outdated, based on the modern development of innovative computer and communication technologies, and theyneed to be clarified. Thus, Jinsil Seo and others explained the impact of modern information processing technologies (including virtual reality technologies) on the transformation of the principles of cybersecurity of enterprises (Jinsil et al., 2019). A similar view is given by Raj Badhwar on the need to revise conservative principles of cybersecurity in conditions of implementation of artificial intelligence technologies (Badhwar, 2021).

Quite a thorough study was conducted by S.F. Lehenchuk et al., who position “integrity”, “confidentiality” and “accessibility” as the principles of cybersecurity of accounting information (Lehenchuk et al., 2021). It is worth noting that the above list of principles is basic, but not complete, as it does not take into account the multifaceted nature of cyber threats to enterprises. In particular, Gurdip Kaur et al. complement the principles of cybersecurity, integrity, confidentiality and accessibility related to the principles of accountability and reliability (Kaur et al., 2021). The same principles, only in a different interpretation, are considered by Anne Kohnke and Dan Shoemaker (2015).

The scientific positioning of commercial secrets in the activities of economic entities directly depends on the development of the market economy and institutional transformations of the society. For developing countries, the concepts of trade secrets and confidentiality of information are inherent. All indicators of financial and economic activity are classified as a secret under conditions of unfair competition, legal unregulation of economic processes, excessive state regulation of enterprises, etc. This encourages management to consider all the information that has nothing to do with the secret as an economic category (Aleksandrov and Polovian, 2000).

In economically developed countries, a part of confidential information that has commercial importance for an enterprise is a trade secret that requires establishment ofeffective cybersecurity. In this case, the accounting system is advisable to be considered from an institutional standpoint as an identifier and differentiator of information that is a trade secret. Through the separation of accounting on financial and management, the information that has a commercial interest for the management of an enterprise and requires limited accessis separated. Therefore, accounting in terms of its division into financial and management has an important mission to determine the list of trade secrets and ensure cyber protection of confidential accounting information.

Legislative consolidation of the division of accounting into financial (public accounting information) and management (limited accounting information) forms the primary legal field for separation of information containing trade secrets. However, the classification from the standpoint of cybersecurity is quite conditional, as financial accounting information can also be confidential. Primary accounting documents and accounts are in most cases common to different types of accounting. In addition, researches on the integration of accounting in conditions of automated processing of accounting information which eliminates some species differences are being conducted more and more actively.

Accounting information about economic, scientific and technical, financial, investment, marketing activity contains trade secrets. The use of accounting information ensures uninterrupted economic activity, obtaining positive financial results and achieving competitive advantages in the market. Getting this information to outsiders can lead to economic losses. In case of the use of accounting information that has lost confidentiality, possible non-compliance with financial and economic plans for tactical and strategic planning of enterprises may arise.

The detailed analytical accounting data can also be used by attackers for causing economic damage or in commercial purposes. When composing and compressing financial accounting data in the accounting registers, later – in the financial statements, the detailed requisites of business transactions are lost. However, the primary data in intermediate analytical tables and documents fully identify the facts of economic events and phenomena, and therefore require limited access. For example, information about suppliers and buyers, delivery dates, popularity of certain products (works, services), cost for innovation and technical development, the state of wear of equipment, etc. may be of interest to competitors.

Additional cyber threats may arise when accounting information reaches attackers during several reporting periods. With the use of the methods of dynamic analysis, it is possible to identify trends in the financial and economic activities of an enterprise. Based on a forecast of business entities development, the strategies for harming an enterprise that has lost confidential information are built.

At the same time, not all information can be recognized as a trade secret, regardless of the will of accounting and management staff. First of all, the constituent information that identifies business entities, their location, founders and owners, areas of economic activity is not subject to classificationas a secret. All types of financial statements, in accordance with the list established by the national legislation of countries or international associations, are public. Similarly, data on the tax base, accrued taxes and fees, as well as debt repayment to fiscal institutions cannot be a commercial secret. Other activities of economic entities related to environmental, social and public interests may not be classified as a secret. The list of accounting information that is prohibited from restricting access may increase for public, financial, investment enterprises, as well as state-owned institutions.

To ensure the protection of confidential information, a company, represented by its management, as the main generator and owner of trade secrets, determines the list of confidential information. In addition, accounting and management professionals have the right to determine the list of persons who may own, deal with, use such information, regulate the rules of information processing and access to it, as well as establish other conditions for trade secrets (Perevalova and Kvasha, 2011).

Effective protection of commercial secrets involves accounting and control of access of persons to confidential information. It is advisable to fixa person, time, place and content of information that is positioned as a commercial secret. In case of loss of confidential accounting information, it is possible to identify a list of suspects, which determines the principle of sanctioning.

Sanctioning in the work with accounting information is controlled through the system of granting rights to transformational actions. That is, with the use of personalized logins and passwords, digital keys, identification of an employee granting of rights for processingrecords is carried out. Sanctioning of information processing is a guarantee for ensuring the integrity of the information model of enterprise operations. Violation of the principle of sanctioning in the processing of accounting information occurs as a result of theft, substitution, selection of means of identification of persons. Unlawful actions lead to unauthorized access to the recordsby third parties, which is not provided by the information regulations of an enterprise.

In order to bring individuals to justice for violating the confidentiality regime, it is necessary to conclude preliminary agreements on non-disclosure of information. Traditionally, a liability agreement is concluded with an employee, which specifies financial sanctions for security breaches, theft, damage to property or non-compliance with functional responsibilities. In case of a breach of contractual relationship regarding the loss of trade secrets, additional disciplinary, administrative and criminal liability of employees may arise.

Disciplinary measures include: reprimand, warning, reproof, transfer to another job, etc. (Syrotiuk, 2010). Administrative liability includes sanctions in the form of fines for a violation, use, disclosure of commercial information in order to cause damage to the business reputation or property of an entrepreneur (Marchuk, 2012). Criminal liability is provided for illegal collection of information for the purpose of commercial espionage and for disclosure of commercial secrets, which leads to possible imprisonment and compensation of material and moral damages to the management of an enterprise (Dykyi and Semenchuk, 2005).

Detection of the fact of loss of confidential information requires automatic delete of the value of trade secrets from the accounts. The fact of cyber threats leads to a decrease in the value of intangible assets, as well as goodwill. It is important to take actions to overcome the effects of cyber threats, which requires a review of new tactics and strategies for an enterprise development. Loss of confidential information foresees informing all persons and entities involved in commercial secrets. It is also necessary to improve the organizational structure of an enterprise, including accounting and security departments. The identification of employees who have violated the security regime requires their prosecution. The speed of action determines the timeliness of ending the impact of cyber risks and minimizing their consequences. Monitoring of the security regime is carried out on the basis of control of access to accounting information, which determines the principle of availability in the cybersecurity of an enterprise.

Availability of accounting information is the ability of accounting professionals and stakeholders to access information at the right time. In conditions of full automation of processing of the accounting information the round-the-clock mode of maintenance of availability is necessary. Availability is realized through the provision of records from a variety of sources on different media. Through communication channels, records are transmitted between stages of their transformation and are displayed to stakeholders. Cyber threats are aimed at blocking access to recirds, which violates the principle of availability.

Quite often, the termination of access to accounting information is due to unintentional factors that have accidental character. For example, power disconnexion or electricity interruptions, Internet outages, hardware or software failures, imperfect business communications, temporary disability, or dismissal of employees responsible for processing records can disrupt availability. Blocking access to records can be the result of intentional actions by attackers. The result of cyberattacks on web resources, databases, communication channels or other types of software and hardware of enterprises is the inability of interested parties to obtain accounting information within a specified period of time.

The consequence of blocking access to accounting information is non-compliance with the time regime of its transmission to the next stage of processing or consumption. The timeliness of the information process is violated and the cycles of accounting information processing are shifted. The time lag between the stages of collecting records and making management decisions can increase to critical values, at which the value of information for stakeholders is lost.

Blocking of information access has catastrophic consequencesespecially for management accounting, which leads to transformation of useful accounting information into absolutely irrelevant data sets. Such data is not useful for users, as it reflects events with a significant time lag. In other words, accounting information is not operational, which levels the benefits of using computer and communication technology.

The principle of **addressness** is connected with the availability of accounting information. Accounting information must be delivered to the place of its consumption in accordance with the time and content requirements. The addressness of accounting information reflects its intended purpose for reaching a specific recipient. Therefore, the direction of accounting data should be considered in conjunction with the classification of stakeholders. Financial accounting information is addressed mainly to external users, management accounting – to external users.

If information is sent to the wrong user, its value is lost. The user can get records that he does not need. Instead, records that are useful to him may be mistakenly addressed to another stakeholder. The purpose of cyberattacks for violatingaddressnessof accounting information is to create communication chaos, which ultimately leads to blocking of useful communications.

Ensuring availability of accounting information requires functioning of the accounting department in a continuous mode. Continuity should be implemented in relation to the following: the work of software and hardware of an enterprise, establishment of communication channels, prevention of power outages, functioning of the personnel of an enterprise, prevention and prompt elimination of consequences of cyberattacks, etc.

In case when it is impossible to block access to the records, cyberattacks focus on harming its integrity. The **integrity** of accounting information is the ability to provide interested parties with complete information in its original form without unauthorized changes. The accounting data that have passed all stages of processing in accordance with the established methodology, internal regulations and rules of the adopted accounting policy, job descriptions of accounting and management specialists are integral. Comprehensive accounting information most fully and accurately corresponds to the social and economic reality in which the company operates, after all processing procedures.

Integrity is directly related to the **completeness** of accounting information, which proves its compliance with the information requests of stakeholders. Complete accounting information is comparable to information needs of its users. Stakeholders can be satisfied only with complete accounting arrays, otherwise accounting information is incomplete. In other words, integrity is the evidence of the complete reliability of information at the time of consumption, which means absence of loss or unauthorized changes to some of its elements.

The reasons for violation of integrity of accounting information are accidental or intentional actions of interested parties. Accidental are mistakes in the work of accounting and management staff of an enterprise, violation of the algorithm or obsolescence of software and hardware, insufficient competence of persons in the process of processing and acquaintance with information are accidental. Intentional actions for violation of integrity of information of an enterprise system are results of cyberattacks by attackers. Third parties may intercept information messages in order to distort them, which will lead to misinformation of stakeholders. Violation of integrity of accounting data may also be the evidence of concealment of violations by personnel of an enterprise or manipulation of information to obtain economic benefits. In particular, based on distortion of financial accounting data, it is possible to attract investors, obtain loans, reduce dividend payments, optimize the accrual and payment of taxes in an illegal manner.

Failure in complying with the principle of integrity in the process of preparing management accounting information can lead to incorrect management. Due to the lack of completeness of accounting information, stakeholders may not have enough information to make management decisions. Management decisions have to be made in conditions of complete or partial uncertainty. Violation of integrity of management accounting information is also a cause of uncertainty among stakeholders about the reliability of the reports provided. To confirm the accuracy of accounting information, a company's management or stakeholders may attract audit services. The task of the audit in such conditions is to provide confidence in the accounting information and conduct a security audit to monitor the state of cybersecurity of an enterprise.

For audit control of cyber protection of accounting information it is necessary to ensure its verifiability. The ability to be verified (the principle of **verifiability**) determines the ability to verify the accuracy of accounting information from various sources. Information that is true is reliable. Accounting and cybersecurity professionals need to have ablity to compare accounting information from a variety of sources, regulatory and legaldocuments, actual social and economic events, etc.

The most complete list of means of ensuring integrity of accounting information wasprovided by S.F.Lehenchuk et al., among which effective measures are:

- formation and use of an adequate system of control of accounting data, which foresees independent means of checks and counterbalances;
- establishment of personal responsibility for accounting specialists for ensuring proper data control;
- development of a mechanism for identifying discrepancies between primary documents, accounts and reports, and the necessary conditions should be created for corrective actions if necessary;
- ensuring proper cyber protection of accounting and other information systems of an enterprise, which are used for the formation of accounting information;
- improving the interface of accounting software in order to implement control functions that provide synchronization and coordination of accounting data in different subsystems;

- use of reliable, stable and secure communication channels for transmission of records (Lehenchuk, 2021).

The relationship of the fundamental principles of cybersecurity of accounting information is shown in Fig. 1.2.

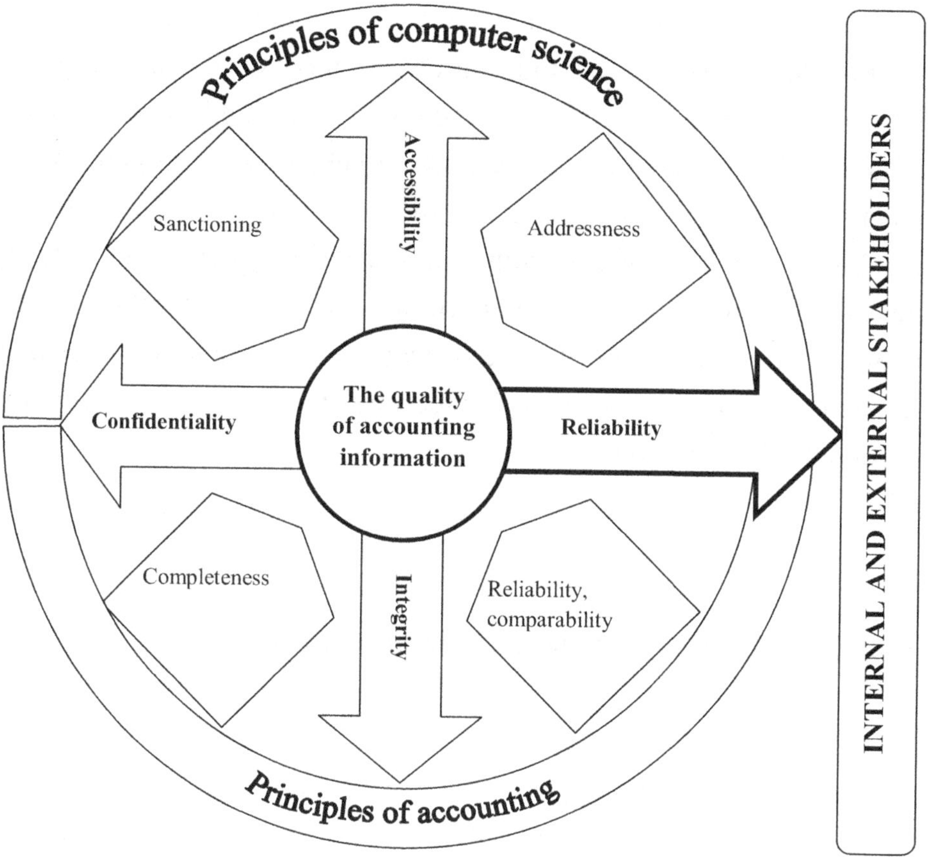

Fig. 1.2. Principles of cybersecurity of accounting information
Source: developed by the authors

The principles of cybersecurity of accounting information are supplemented by other principles of fundamental scientific theories. On the outer radius of the conceptual combination of the basic principles of cybersecurity of accounting information (confidentiality, accessibility, integrity) are the theoretical principles of accounting and the principles of computer science. Adherence to all these principles of cybersecurity ensures the reliability of accounting information. Reliability is the property of information to be unmistakable, independent, unprejudiced, adequate to social and conomic realities. Reliability is a super principle in cybersecurity, which testifies the absence of errors, distortions, inaccuracies caused by third parties, it guarantees the availability and confidentiality of accounting informationas well as. Only reliable information can be used unconditionally by stakeholders. The principle of reliability is formed at the intersection of subject areas of other principles. Obtaining reliable accounting information is the ultimate goal of the combined operation of accounting and security systems. With the further development of computer and communication technologies and the evolutionary complexity of cyber threats, it is possible to supplement the fundamental principles of cybersecurity to ensure the reliability of accounting information.

1.3. Classification of cyber risks in accounting

Since the accounting system is the generator of most economic processes in the enterprise, what cybersecurity requires foremost is accounting information. The variability of cyber threats is growing because of the increasingly complex accounting processes and improvements in computer communication processes. Theft of accounting data, especially that pertaining to trade secrets, has been the most common manifestation of external cyber threats. Internal threats to enterprise informational security are associated with malicious manipulations of accounting data aimed at gaining economic benefits or concealing certain actions or events.

The development of electronic communications has contributed to the spread of computer viruses geared towards harming the accounting system and enterprise management. The number of cyber threats associated with the installation of malicious software to gain unauthorized access to accounting data has gradually risen. Increasingly, the accounting system is becoming the target of cyber threats not only in its capacity as a communication channel for access to critical infrastructure of the enterprise, but also as the method of processing and transmitting accounting information. Popularity of social networks and messengers leads to an increased likelihood of accounting data being leaked to third parties. Consequently, direct cyberattacks against the enterprise accounting system are becoming more frequent. Fraudulent actions of third parties related to obtaining illegal economic benefits have become even more widespread.

Improvement in the methods of executing hybrid conflicts alone results in more complex, permanent, extensive and varied cyber threats. The success of cyberattacks is ensured by using a set of different cyber threats aimed at maximizing the damage done to a business entity. Such threats to information security are detected continuously, which requires the enterprise to create a specialized unit or hire staff specializing in cybersecurity and integrate them into the organizational structure. Therefore, ensuring effective cybersecurity of accounting data necessitates the study of cyber risks grouped according to various classification features.

Scientific and journalistic sources of information on cybersecurity of enterprises use a generally accepted classification of cyber risks. Namely, commonly recognized types of cyber risks include malicious software and viruses, web attacks, web application attacks, phishing, hardware failure, spam, botnet attacks, data breaches, insider threats, data leakage, information leakage, identity theft, cryptojacking, extortionist programs, cyber espionage and others.

For example, the journalistic indexing publishing house The 2019 Kearney Global Services Location Index (2020) uses a simplified classification of cyber risks into: Hacking, Malware, Social, Error, Physical, Misuse (Fig. 1.3).

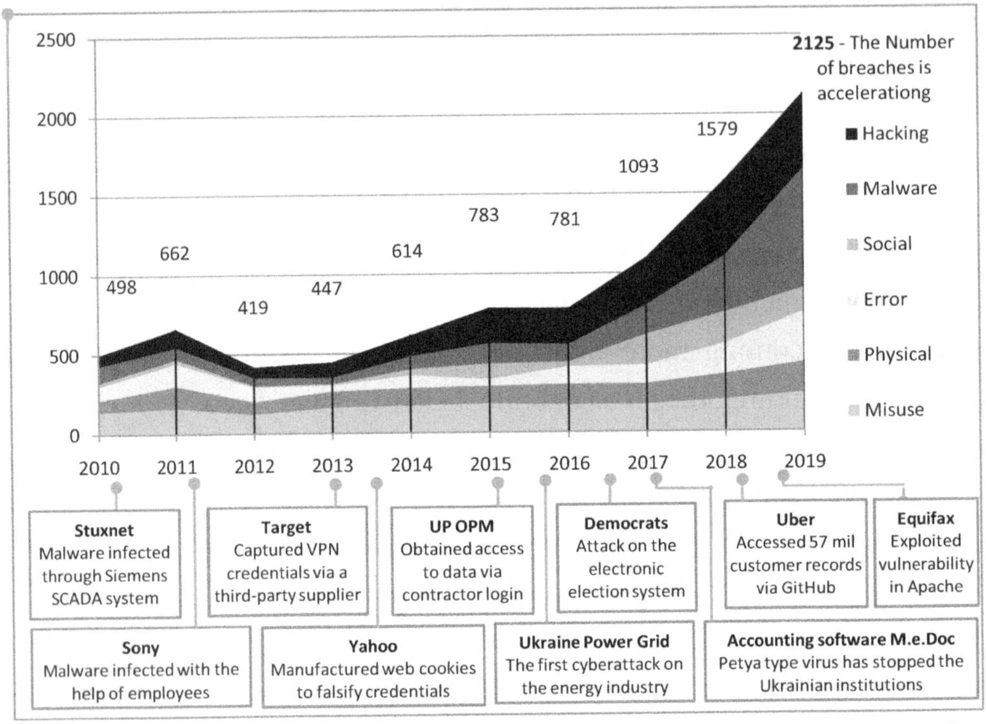

Fig. 1.3. Classification of Large-scale cyber threats (2010-2019)
Source: (2019 Kearney Global Services Location Index, 2020)

The number of large-scale cyberattacks related to outsourcing increased from 498 to 2125 incidents over 10 years (2010-2019). Among the notable attacks, we can highlight the one on the energy sector of Ukraine in 2016 done through the systems of accounting for utility payments, and the spread of the Petya encoder virus through the update of accounting software in Ukraine in 2017 (2019 Kearney Global Services Location Index, 2020). The cyber risks growing in accounting system requires positioning an accounting as the basis for enterprises cybersecurity. Pandemic expectations and the associated distancing of work duties have led to a transformation of priorities in the execution of cyber threats. The method of inflicting damage to cybersecurity of business entities has also changed due to the complexity of information processes at the enterprise.

The current classification of cyber risks and their manifestation during the COVID-19 pandemic is shown in Fig. 1.4.

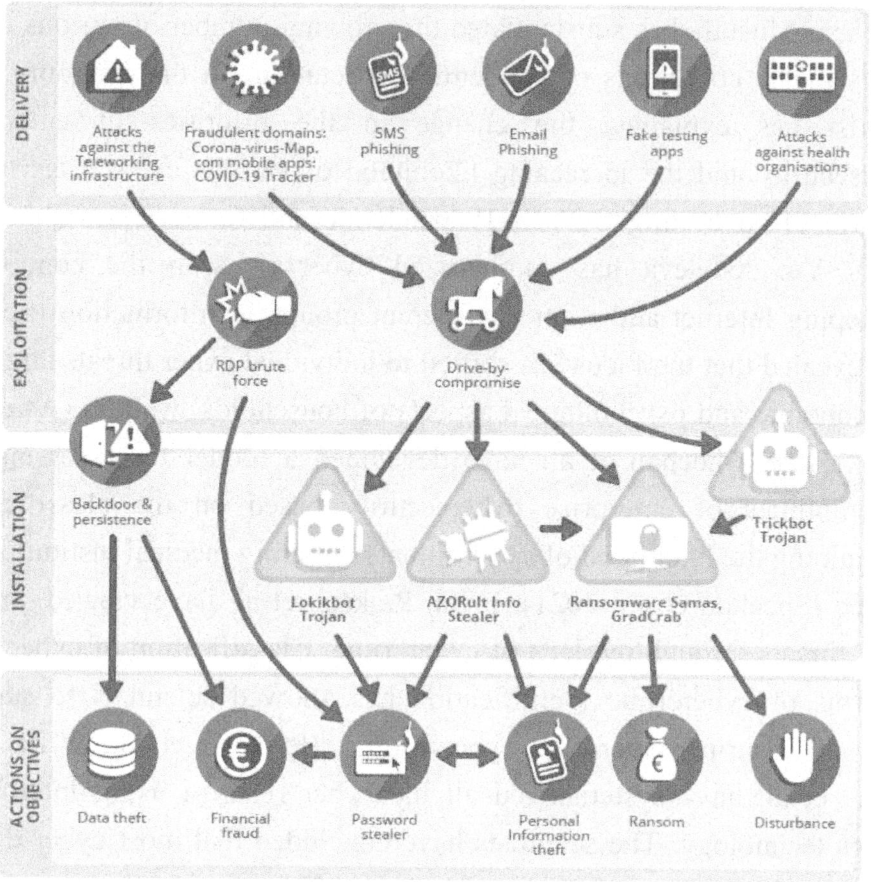

Fig. 1.4. Cyber risks under the conditions of the COVID-19 pandemic
Source: (Main incidents in the EU and worldwide, 2020)

Official statistics use the classification of cyber risks by form and methods of execution. Such grouping of cyber threats is uninformative for the purposes of organizing the cybersecurity of enterprises. Back in 2012,

Michael Schmitt classified cyber conflicts as part of international hostilities with the identification of various cyber threats to the operation of enterprises (Schmitt, 2012). William Steingartner and Darko Galinec have continued this research and created a classification of cyber threats that helped to identify information risks in some countries exerting hybrid influence over others (Steingartner and Galinec, 2021).

Nasir Mustafa has substantiated the growing number of various cyber threats in the conditions of pandemic expectations in the economy. The scientist has explained the change in the priorities of enterprise cybersecurity and the increasing likelihood of various cyber risks in the scenario of continuing COVID-19 pandemic and future crises (Mustafa, 2020). Yu. Asieieva has summarized cyber risks in the context of developing Internet addiction in different groups of information users. It was revealed that the focus has shifted to individual cyber threats targeting the economic and psychological aspects of households' welfare (Asieieva, 2020). Barry Sheehan et al. have developed a model for assessing the vulnerabilities of enterprise cybersecurity based on the classification determining the likelihood of cyber threats targeting medical institutions in Europe (Sheehan et al., 2021). Febin Prakash et al. have viewed various cyber threats through the lens of cybercrime. Classification of cyber risks in terms of cybercrime identification has allowed scientists to suggest ways of ensuring enterprise cybersecurity (Prakash et al., 2019). Md Haque et al. have systematized all the cyber risks of using Internet of Things technology. The scientists have concluded that most cyber threats can be avoided provided that the Internet of Things technology is used in conjunction with effective methods of information protection (Haque et al., 2021). Similarly, R. V. Baranenko has chosen the classification features of cyber threats based on the distinction between "cyberattacks" and "cyberterrorism" (Baranenko, 2021).

The producing nature of accounting, which is the main generator of economic information at the micro-level, has been considered even less in the classification of cyber threats. There are only isolated works on distinguishing various cyber threats in the context of cybersecurity of accounting information. In particular, V. A. Shpak has developed the basic components of comprehensive enterprise cybersecurity in terms of legal, technical, software and organizational measures (Shpak, 2015). Given that collection of accounting information is the first stage of the accounting information process, the system of accounting reporting and data processing of the enterprise is often vulnerable and subjected to active cyber threats. Accounting reports are the basis for recording financial and economic processes in the prescribed forms - documents. The transfer of documents between the sender and the recipient is determined by a certain sequence, which is called document flow. All stages of reporting and document flow of accounting data are vulnerable to specific cyber threats, which can be grouped into:

-loss of the document or its components (appendices, explanations, individual letters or copies) due to theft or voluntary leaks to attackers;

-replacement of documents with similar (analogous) items with distorted data for the purpose of falsification or infliction of economic damage;

-violation of the integrity of the document, which limits its informational value;

- errors when working with documents during their creation and transfer;

-deletion of documents to cause informational and economic damage to the enterprise (Shpak, 2015).

However, the scientist reduces most cyber risks to the violation of reporting and data processing procedures without taking into account the multifaceted nature of threats to information and economic security of enterprises.

In contrast to the research of cyber threats relevant to accounting documents, Gyung Min Lee et al. have investigated the idea of gradually growing risks of fileless and, accordingly, document-less cyberattacks (Lee et al., 2020). As the digitalization of the economy increases, the need for paper and electronic documents abates. Modern cyberattacks are increasingly threatening electronic accounting databases.

S. A. Viter and I. I. Svitlyshyn have systematized the basic principles (software support, protection of confidential information, personal responsibility, secrecy, completeness, access control) by classifying cyber threats and measures (organizational, technical and personnel) to ensure cybersecurity of accounting data (Viter and Svitlyshyn, 2017). However, some of their cybersecurity postulates apply to all information processes and only partially take into account the accounting specifics of economic processes. Similarly, V. M. Rozheliuk divides cyber threats into internal and external and distinguishes different sub-types relevant to accounting (Rozheliuk, 2013). However, the study does not sufficiently take into account the multifaceted nature of accounting cybersecurity. Having summarized the scientific proposals of more than twenty scientists on the definition of "cyber risks", Grzegorz Strupczewski concluded that no studies comprehensively classify the threats to the enterprise accounting systems (Strupczewski, 2021).

We find it prudent to agree with S.M. Denha and Yu. O. Veryha, who state that cyber threats to accounting should primarily be divided into two categories: intentional (fraud and sabotage) and accidental (errors and malfunctions) (Denha and Veryha, 2004). Intentional cyber threats are targeted activities to cause economic and information damage to the business entity. Intentional actions are always planned, premeditated and focused on achieving a clear goal, whereas accidental cyber threats are the result of unintentional errors made by the accounting personnel, an inefficient enterprise accounting system, imperfect information security, poor accounting policies at the enterprise, software and hardware malfunctions, etc. Such threats do not depend on the actions of attackers and lead to unforeseen loss (deletion) of accounting information or creation of favourable conditions for the manifestation of other cyber threats as a result of chance.

Intentional cyber threats can be divided into active and passive ones. Active threats entail inflicting harm on the enterprise or receiving economic gain through manipulation of accounting information. Active threats to the information security of the enterprise manifest in the form of cyberattacks and virus interventions, information fraud, insider sabotage and unauthorized transfer of accounting data. Instead, passive cyber threats are associated with unauthorized access to accounting data. They are usually latent, as they focus on adapting and integrating into the informational space of the enterprise for a long time.

Active and passive cyber threats to accounting should not be directly associated with the internal and external environment of the enterprise. Depending on the spatial manifestation of cyber threats with regards to the information system of the enterprise, it is advisable to distinguish between internal, intra-system and external types of threats. Threats differ in their origin and subjectivity of cyber risks. If the employees or owners (founders) of the enterprise are the cause of the cybersecurity violation, then the cyber risks are internal. Cyber threats are intra-system if they are initiated by persons who are not employed by the enterprise, but participate in a two-way information exchange with the accounting system. These include counterparties, controlling institutions, audit and consulting firms, banking and credit institutions, etc. External cyber threats come from the external environment and are caused by persons informationally and financially unrelated to the enterprise.

The principle of classifying cyber risks of the accounting system according to the criterion of location is similar. Depending on the relation between the location of the cyber threats' instigators and the business entity targeted by the cyberattack, cyber risks are divided into internal (instigators are on the premises of the business entity); regional (in the city, region, state); national (in the country, associations of countries); international (instigators are abroad) risks.

However, cyber threats to accounting information are not always related to the activities of certain insiders or outsiders. Cyber risks quite often arise from other sources due to inaction or errors (malfunctions) of software and hardware. Accordingly, the sources of threat to the accounting system may include human activities, inaction of systems and technologies, or errors in information processes. Ineffective operation of software and hardware can lead to accidental leakage of confidential information, suspension of economic activity and emergence of “weak spots” in the cybersecurity system of the enterprise. Gaps in the cybersecurity of the enterprise information system, as well as errors in the algorithm for processing accounting information can be used by attackers to commit illegal acts.

This classification of cyber risks can be supplemented by grouping them by origin. Using the origin of cyber threats as the classification criterion, they are divided into:

- those associated with the loss (damage, leakage, concealment, deletion) of accounting data;
- those associated with the content of information files (incorporation of inaccurate, incomplete, substituted, distorted accounting data);
- those associated with informational influence (dissemination of false, negative accounting information to informationally influence owners, employees, contractors, etc. of the enterprise) (Zinkevich and Shtatov, 2007).

Identification of the sources of cyber threats contributes to the development of scenarios for their mitigation. Measures for preventive cyber protection of enterprises can be developed on the basis of the created scenarios of cyber threats manifestation, taking into account the individual characteristics of enterprise operation.

However, the cybersecurity of enterprises is much more reliant on the classification of cyber risks according to the goal (threat to information or information system of the enterprise). The goal of information cyber threats is to manipulatively gain access to accounting data. The information infrastructure remains beyond the consideration of attackers. Meanwhile, threats to the information system of the enterprise are focused on obtaining benefits or harming businesses; in such case, accounting data is used only as a means of gaining access to the informational space of the enterprise.

When classifying cyber risks, the goal system is divided into target groups related to software, hardware, personnel, regulatory and organizational support. Each type of threat is associated with ineffectiveness or low effectiveness of certain components of cybersecurity. For example, software threats are the result of errors in the installation and operation of computer programs created for automated processing of accounting data. Hardware threats are related to obsolescence or inefficient use of accounting automation hardware. Personnel threats are caused by insufficient professionalism of accounting staff, as well as the impossibility of training (retraining) and lack of motivation to use modern computer and communication technologies. Regulatory threats emerge due to the lack of opportunities to adapt automated accounting to the requirements of internal and external regulations. Organizational threats are associated with shortcomings in the organizational structure of the enterprise and the accounting department, which lead to accidental errors and vulnerabilities of the information system of the enterprise.

It is advisable to develop measures to prevent and eliminate cyber threats in accordance with the target classification. Therefore, it is necessary to use software, hardware, personnel, regulatory and organizational measures of cybersecurity.

The level of damage is related to the number of instigators and targets of cyber threats. According to the scale of cyber threats, they should be classified into: (a) general, which threaten the operation of the business entity as a whole; (b) local, which single out directions or areas of activity (operational, administrative, sales, financial, investment, etc.) of the enterprise; (c) targeted, focusing on individual accounting targets (noncurrent assets, cash, income, etc.).

At the same time, cyber threats must be classified according to the criterion of aspect. In terms of the aspects of cybersecurity of the accounting system, cyber threats should be grouped into: (a) threats to confidentiality (accounting data is accessed by persons without proper authorization); (b) threats to integrity (accounting data is distorted, destroyed or replaced); (c) availability threats (access to accounting data is restricted or blocked).

Different aspects of cyber threats are realized through a various forms of assaults. According to the form of manifestation of cyber risks, we can distinguish cyberattacks, cyber incidents, cyber espionage, cyberterrorism, and cyber wars, which have different motivations for cyber intervention and different methods of implementation. The national legislation of Ukraine defines cyberattack as "targeted (intentional) action in cyberspace, which is carried out by means of electronic communications (including information and communication technologies, software, hardware, other technical and technological means and equipment) and focused on achieving one or a combination of such goals: violation of confidentiality, integrity, availability of electronic information processed (transmitted, stored) in communication and / or technological systems, obtaining unauthorized access to such resources; violation of security, sustainable, reliable and regular operation of communication and / or technological systems; use of the communication system, its resources and means of electronic communications for cyberattacks on other subjects of cybersecurity" (Pro osnovni zasady zabezpechennia kiberbezpeky Ukrainy,

2017). Cyberattacks are fundamentally different from other manifestations of cyber risks. A cyber incident is a single event or a set of accidental adverse events of an unintentional nature that damage the enterprise's accounting system. Cyber espionage is unauthorized continuous multiple covert theft of accounting data. Cyberterrorism is terrorist activity aimed at malicious manipulation of accounting data and causing harm to the enterprise. Cyberwar is the destabilization of enterprise information systems and the use of accounting systems to create chaos in the economic activities of enterprises and people.

Forms of cyber threats to accounting differ in latency and duration of information intervention, which can also be used as classification criteria. In particular, cyberattacks and cyber incidents are visible and short-lived, cyber espionage is covert and long-term (or permanent), cyberterrorism and cyberwar are aggressive and long-term.

Moreover, all cyber risks can be classified into criminal and non-criminal (Volosovych and Klapkiv, 2018). The classification criterion is the interpretation of cyber threats from the standpoint of criminal liability for their execution. The criminal risks of the accounting system are associated with illegal activities (hacker attacks, physical attacks, blackmail and fraud). All other cyber threats in the form of anthropogenic or technological errors and force majeure are considered non-criminal.

The consideration of legality of cyber threats to accounting makes it possible to identify the consequences of interfering in the cybersecurity of enterprises. According to the end result, cyber threats can be divided into those affecting information processes, causing difficulties in the operation of the accounting system, and destroying the enterprise management system. Non-criminal cyber threats mainly result in the theft or distortion of accounting data, while criminal cyber risks are focused on blocking certain information systems or interfering with the operation of business entities. Thus, the risks that cause difficulties in the operation of the accounting system and block the management system are destructive for the company.

Such cyber threats require a balanced approach to the organization of cybersecurity in terms of avoiding destructive risks. To successfully prevent cyber threats, it is important to determine their probability. Classification according to the probability of the cyber threats can divide them into unlikely, probable and inevitable ones. Thus, it is recommended to assess all cyber threats to accounting in terms of the probability of their manifestation in order to ensure effective cybersecurity of the enterprise. If necessary, the probabilistic classification of cyber threats can be expanded by using a larger number of categories depending on the ranges of probability: no probability (coefficient of occurrence - 0), low probability (0.1-0.3), average probability (0, 4-0.5), high probability (0.6-0.8), guaranteed onset (0.9-0.99), imminent onset (1).

The classification of cyber threats to accounting in the context of various classification criteria is generalized in Table 1.2. Measures to organize the cybersecurity of accounting information change depending on the type of cyber threats listed in the table and relevance for a particular business entity.

Table 1.2

Generalized classification of cyber threat to accounting data

No.	**Classification criterion**	**Type of cyber threat**
1	**2**	**3**
1.	Intent	- accidental, - intentional.
2.	Mode	- active, - passive.
3.	Information and financial interest	- internal, - intra-system, - external.
4.	Location	- internal, - regional, - national, - international.

1	2	3
5.	Instigator	- human actions, - inactivity of systems and technologies, - errors in information processes.
6.	Origin	those associated with: - loss of data, - creation of information file, - information influence.
7.	Goal	- threats to accounting data, - threats to the information system of the enterprise.
8.	Target	- software support, - hardware support, - personnel support, - regulatory support, - organizational support.
9.	Scale	- general, - local, - targeted.
10.	Aspect	- threats to confidentiality, - threats to integrity, - availability threats.
11.	Form of manifestation	- cyberattack, - cyber espionage, - cyber incident, - cyber terrorism, - cyber war.
12.	Legality	- criminal (hacker attacks, physical attacks, blackmail and fraud), - non-criminal (anthropogenic errors, technological errors, force majeure).
13.	Duration	- short-term, - long-term, - continuous.
14.	Latency	- covert, - visible, - aggressive.
15.	Probability	- unlikely, - probable, - inevitable.
16.	Consequences	- influencing information processing, - causing difficulties in the operation of the accounting system, - destroying the enterprise management system.

Source: systemized and improved by the author.

Cyber threats can also be classified by gender and age of cybercriminals. In particular, according to statistics, 67% of cyber threats are perpetrated by male criminals (age: up to 25 years - 13%, 25-40 years -

39%, over 40 years - 15%) and, accordingly, 33% are perpetrated by women (age: up to 25 years - 6%, 25-40 years - 20%, more than 40 years - 7%) (Pidsumky 2018 roku v tsyfrakh, 2018).

The relevance of age and gender distribution for the classification of cyber threats is substantiated in the research of Ioannis Tsimperidis et al. (2021). However, such a classification is not very useful in developing measures to ensure the cybersecurity of accounting data, as it involves the identification and division of cybercriminals, rather than cyber risks.

The suggested classification of cyber threats should be used in the organization of constant cybersecurity of enterprises. Each type of cyber threats to accounting data requires a specific method of prevention, avoidance and elimination of consequences. As a result, cybersecurity is a dynamic and adaptive process that takes into account the differences in the manifestation of different cyber threats. Since the complexity of information processes and the advancements in computer and communication technologies are continuously changing along with socio-economic conditions of enterprise operation, the proposed classification of cyber threats to accounting data will need to be amended and supplemented.

1.4. Innovative accounting methodology of ensuring the interaction of economic and cybersecurity of enterprises

Most cyber risks inherent to the activities of economic entities are associated with the theft of accounting information or reduction of its quality parameters. The economic security of the enterprise is ensured by complying with the qualitative requirements to accounting information. The quality of information depends on its compliance with the expectations of stakeholders. Violation of any of the quality parameters of the accounting system can lead to loss of its usefulness and, consequently, economic significance for internal and external users. In most cases, the enterprise suffers economic losses if incorrect accounting information is in operation. Management decisions based on false (distorted or corrupted) accounting information cause damage to the economic security.

The actions of internal users operating accounting information are related to the economic activities of the enterprise, while the external users affect the functioning of other economic entities. Thus, non-compliance with the qualitative parameters of the accounting system causes economic damages twice: first, through direct losses due to the actions or inaction of managers (owners and founders) and, second, through indirect losses or lost economic benefits that could have been extracted from cooperation with external stakeholders. As a result, there is a direct link between economic and cybersecurity of enterprises. In practice, the relationship between economic and security activities involves the study of accounting mechanisms to identify the impact of cyber threats on the economic security of the enterprise.

At the enterprise level, economic security characterizes the current level of protection of the enterprise's most important interests from unfair competition, excessive pressure from regulatory authorities, incompetent decisions, imperfect regulatory framework, as well as the ability of the enterprise to withstand information threats (Horbachenko, 2020). The impact of cyber risks on enterprise economic security is the subject of scientific research of many scholars. In particular, B. Rodrigues et al. (2019) argue that the need to ensure cybersecurity is a side effect of digitalization of the economy. According to the scientists, it is important to develop effective measures to prevent and eliminate cyber risks by predicting the economic consequences of cybersecurity breaches.

B. Rajput considers the phenomenon of “cybercrime in the economic sector”, which has arisen in recent years due to the connection between cyber risks and economic consequences of their manifestation. The scientist concludes that due to the increasing integration of economic and cyber space, the number of such crimes will continue to grow (Rajput, 2020). Exploring the economic consequences of various cyber risks, Yu. Shitova and Y. Shitov point out that all modern cybercrime focuses on obtaining certain economic benefits: global espionage, financial attacks, card fraud, information theft and phishing, network attacks and traffic interception to steal intellectual property, cryptographers and extortionists, cryptojacking, etc (Shitova and Shitov, 2019).

Researchers have also investigated ways to ensure enterprise cybersecurity in terms of minimizing economic losses of the enterprise. For example, S. Horbachenko has substantiated the expediency of creating a single national cybersecurity system, which would unite the information space of enterprises into a single integrated system that would be a full-fledged component of national security at the state level (Horbachenko, 2020). R. Marasigan has highlighted the importance of instigating institutional changes in the economy at the micro and macro levels to overcome cyber barriers and threats to the operation of enterprises (Marasigan, 2019). K. Wilson and J. Hugh have identified the organizational, methodological, software and hardware support critically important for a cybersecurity system, which is crucial for ensuring sustainable economic security of the enterprise (Wilson and Hugh, 2014).

R. Rue and S. Pfleeger have proposed different models of economic assessment of cyber risks. Scientists have explained the various mechanisms of cybersecurity's impact on the economic condition of the enterprise in terms of determining the economic losses resulting from the manifestation of cyber risks (Rue and Pfleeger, 2009). Similarly, W. Patterson and M. Gergely have developed a method for determining the economic efficiency of enterprise cybersecurity and its setup by analysing the impact of cyber risks on economic losses or costs (capital and current) of the enterprise (Patterson and Gergely, 2020). Thus, most scientists associate the need for cybersecurity with the growing pervasiveness of information and communication technologies in information processes. However, the connection between intensification of cybersecurity and increasing implementation of information processing technologies in social and economic processes has been refuted by the analysis using global rating data (Global Cybersecurity Index, 2018) (Fig. 1.5).

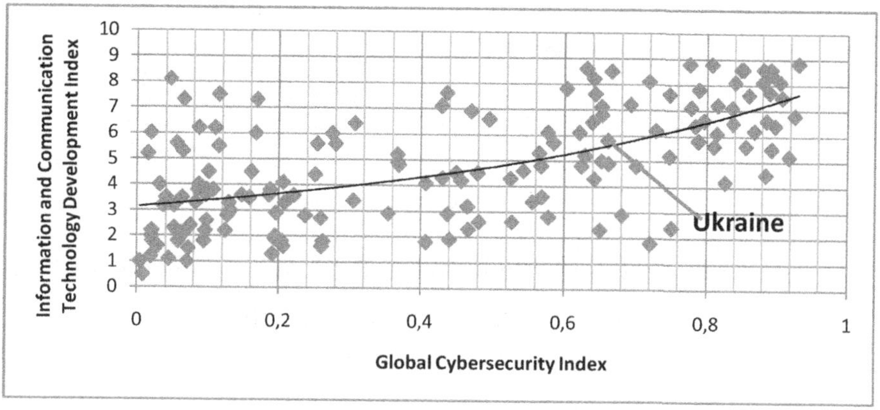

Fig. 1.5. The relationship between the level of cybersecurity and ICT development of countries

Source: calculated on the basis of (Global Cybersecurity Index, 2018)

The approximate and smoothed trend line built using data on the relationship between the index of ICT development and the index of cybersecurity makes it possible to identify an imbalance between these indicators for many countries. Significant positional deviation of the values from the average trend line shown in Fig. 1.5 shows the lack of a direct relationship between the development of ICT and the level of cybersecurity in most countries.

A more homogeneous result was obtained when comparing the ratio of the cybersecurity index alternately with the innovation index (Fig. 1.6) and the connectivity index (Fig. 1.7). Thus, the increased attention to measures of ensuring cybersecurity is precipitated by innovations and connectivity at the micro and macro levels. The more innovations are introduced and the more network infrastructure develops in national socio-economic processes, the bigger the need for an effective cybersecurity system.

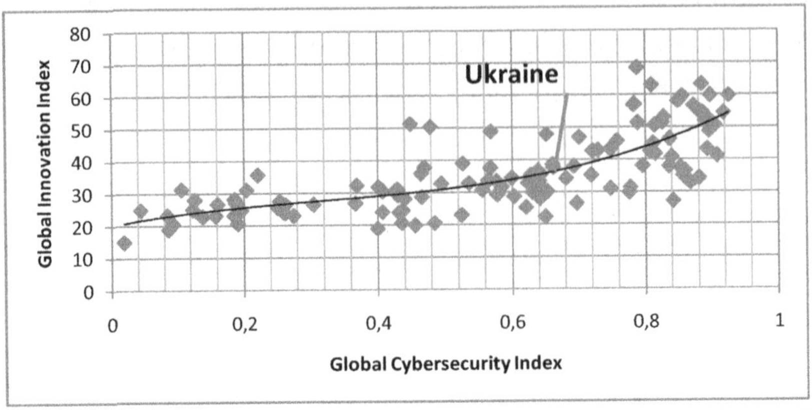

Fig. 1.6. The relationship between the level of cybersecurity and the level of innovation of countries

Source: calculated on the basis of (Global Innovation Index, 2018; Global Cybersecurity Index, 2018)

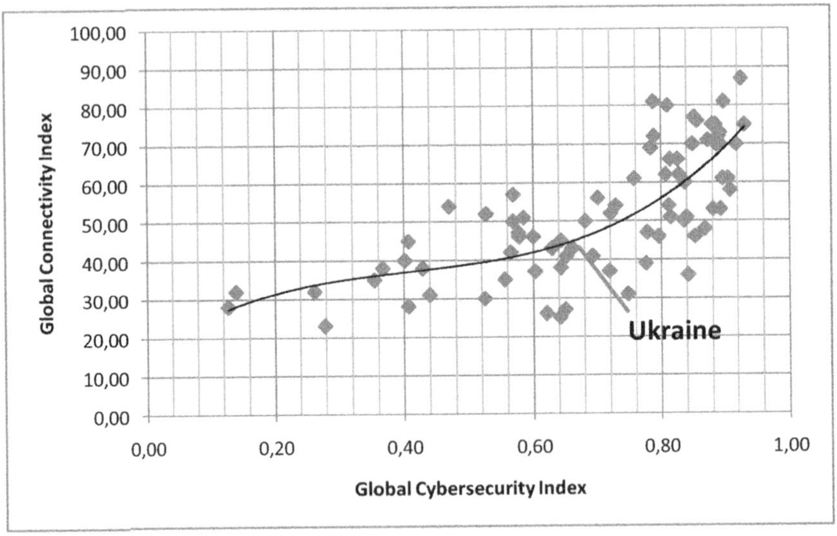

Fig. 1.7. The relationship between the state of cybersecurity and connectivity of countries

Source: calculated on the basis of (Global Connectivity Index, 2018; Global Cybersecurity Index, 2018)

The level of innovation and development of network infrastructure determines the digital competitiveness of the country. Fig. 1.8 shows a direct relationship between the level of cybersecurity and digital competitiveness of countries, as evidenced by only slight deviations of analytical data from the average trend line. It should be noted that some countries with low indicators of innovation and digitalization of socio-economic processes occupy high positions in the ranking of cybersecurity. For example, Ukraine's indicators: Innovation Index - 38.52; Connectivity index - 43; Digital Competitiveness Index - 51.29, all with a fairly high Cybersecurity Index of 0.661, which is explained by the need to combat ongoing cyber threats due to hybrid foreign influence.

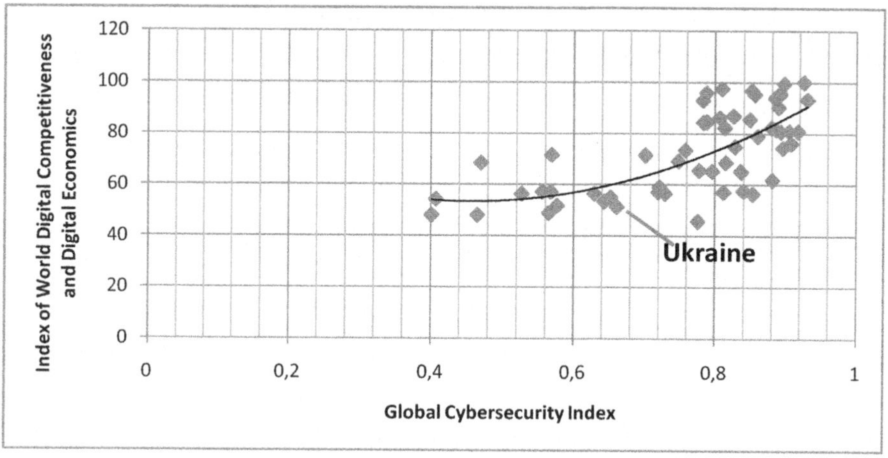

Fig. 1.8. The relationship between the level of cybersecurity and the digital competitiveness of countries

Source: calculated on the basis of (World Digital Competitiveness Ranking, 2018; Global Cybersecurity Index, 2018)

The digital competitiveness of countries is the basis for the development of a digital economy. When most socio-economic processes are digitized, their cybersecurity must be ensured. Accounting is the information basis for the digital economy. Accounting data becomes an important target of cybersecurity in the terms of the relationship with the national economic security, various industries and individual economic entities.

Yu.Yu. Moroz and Yu.S. Tsal-Tsalko have defined cybersecurity in terms of the accounting policy of the enterprise based on ensuring the economic security of the enterprise. They have defined it as the protection of vital interests and accounting information of the enterprise from internal and external threats, i.e. protection of the enterprise, its human and intellectual potential, technologies, profits, added and market value, which is provided by a system of special legal, economic, organizational, information, technical and social measures (Moroz and Tsal-Tsalko, 2017). V. A. Nekhai and V. V. Nekhai consider information security an important component of economic security, which requires accounting information to be cyber secured for its quality parameters to be met (Nekhai et al., 2017).

V. V. Yevdokymov overviews reliability, the qualitative characteristic of accounting information, in the context of ensuring the economic security of the enterprise (Yevdokymov, 2011). Reliability, in his opinion, is a characteristic of information that provides confidence in the appropriateness of its assumptions about errors and trends, as well as the truth of intentions to provide all data in a veritable form; it meets the principles of verifiability, credibility and neutrality. In addition, it should be noted that ensuring the reliability of accounting information in the digital economy primarily involves the ability of accounting systems to avoid and resist cyber threats. However, such studies have been partial and fragmentary, not allowing authors to establish the multifaceted nature of the connection between economic and cybersecurity of enterprises.

The idea of accounting's important socio-economic role and significance is at the core of the innovative approach to the theoretical and methodological principles of accounting. The hypothesis of innovative nature of accounting as a set of methods to ensure the interaction of economic and cybersecurity of enterprises has been posited.

Accounting principles are its fundamental basis. The study of accounting principles allows us to identify empirical relationships, patterns of development and features of accounting, which is influenced by current trends in information and communication technologies development. It is possible to substantiate the interaction between economic and cybersecurity of enterprises by analysing accounting principles. The increasing number and difficulty of cyber risks require continuous adaptation and transformation of accounting principles to internal and external conditions of enterprise's operation. The ways of practically implementing (adhering to) them are optimized in order to ensure the economic security of the enterprise. As a result, cyber risks exert direct and reverse influence on the financial and economic performance of economic entities through accounting principles. Table 1.3 presents the peculiarities of adhering to fundamental accounting principles in the conditions of simultaneously ensuring economic and cybersecurity, which is the first fundamental methodological level of their interaction.

Adherence to the fundamental principles of accounting allows the enterprise to implement its functions to ensure the proper quality of accounting information. The quality of information produced by accounting depends on its ability to meet the requirements and expectations of internal and external users. Cyber risks are aimed at reducing or negating the usefulness of accounting information due to non-compliance with its quality parameters. The proper quality of accounting information determines the quality of the interaction between economic and cybersecurity of enterprises. The main qualitative parameters of accounting data, which are targeted by cyber risks, are credibility, timeliness, availability, feasibility, reliability, comparability and others.

Table 1.3

Adherence to the principles of accounting and financial reporting in terms of ensuring economic and cybersecurity

No.	Principles of accounting and financial reporting	Manifested risks to economic and cybersecurity in case of non-compliance	Information consequences of cyber threats	Economic consequences of cyber threats
1.	Transparency	Accounting information is distorted or substituted in the process of its transfer to internal and external users due to incomplete (unreliable) reflection of financial and economic operations in the system of accounts and reports.	Falsification of accounting data when transmitting to internal and external users	Enterprise employees or third parties obtaining economic benefits
2.	Autonomy	Enterprise loses information independence and autonomy due to unauthorized breaches of the information system by a third party for continuous monitoring of information processes in accounting and management.	Continuous unauthorized access to accounting data	Industrial espionage, reduced economic independence
3.	Orderliness	Managerial decisions are ill-timed due to violation of the order of preparation and submission of data and implementation of accounting policies	Ill-timed processing of accounting data	Violation of management timeliness
4.	Continuity	The financial and economic activity of the enterprise is blocked, suspended (disrupted); the enterprise is brought to bankruptcy.	Blocking of information flows	Decrease in market value, raider capture, unfair competition
5.	Accountability	Revenues are underreported or expenditures are overstated to avoid taxes, paying dividends, etc.	Falsification of accounting data to avoid creditor obligations	Financial losses of economically connected stakeholders-creditors
6.	Prevalence of essence over form	Accounting data is distorted at the time of its initial recording by misrepresenting the nature of economic operations.	Falsification of accounting data at the time of its initial recording	Enterprise employees or third parties obtaining economic benefits
7.	Single monetary unit	Risks of electronic transactions are increased due to substitution of fiat money with cryptocurrency outside national currency systems to ensure confidentiality of monetary operations.	Hacker attacks to access electronic money services	Theft of funds

Source: created by the authors.

Regardless of the information subordination of qualitative parameters of accounting data or their grouping by various classification criteria, the economic security of the enterprise depends on the frequency of cyber threats. In particular, cyber risks are focused on reducing the quality of accounting information through: credibility – making incorrect (erroneous) management decisions; timeliness – making belated management decisions; accessibility – inability to obtain or perceive information in the process of making management decisions; feasibility – blocking the necessary management decisions; reliability – inability to make management decisions due to lack of trust in information; comparability – making unreasonable management decisions due to inability to assess and analyse accounting indicators; other qualitative parameters of accounting data – damage to the management of the enterprise. Thus, the manifestation of cyber risks is the reason for reduced efficiency of the management system, which leads to the enterprise suffering economic damage.

All qualitative parameters of accounting data are ultimately related to its confidentiality in terms of ensuring economic and cybersecurity of the enterprise. Accounting data is nominally divided into public and confidential on the distinction between financial and managerial accounting. Identification of accounting items and its division into types determines the methodical level of the interaction between economic and cybersecurity of the enterprise.

Confidentiality of managerial accounting data is precipitated by the exclusively internal use and need to ensure that unauthorized persons do not get access to it. Lack of proper cybersecurity for managerial accounting data can lead to third parties using it to gain a competitive advantage in the market, attract buyers and suppliers on more favourable commercial terms, optimize technological side of operations, revise personnel, pricing, sales policy, etc. Violation of confidentiality ultimately leads to economic losses for the enterprise. Economic damages caused by the manifestation of cyber risks are associated with losing operating profits due to loss of markets, suspension of operation, disruption of logistics cycles, disruptions to the rhythm of production, loss of intellectual property.

Additionally, the use of false internal accounting information may lead to erroneous management decisions. On higher level of management the larger potential economic losses from making incorrect management decisions. The greatest threat to the economic security of the enterprise may be posed by ineffective strategic management caused by the use of accounting data altered by cyber attacks.

The intensity and frequency of cyber threats also depends on the type of the accounting item. In particular, most cyberattacks are aimed at stealing money and its equivalents. Cyber threats are equally likely to manifest in relation to the production and related calculations and manufacturing technologies (performance of works, provision of services) and fixed assets of the enterprise to damage critical infrastructure and suspend the enterprise operations, etc. However, accounting items such as inventories and small current assets are rarely cyber-threatened.

Although financial accounting information is not a trade secret, it also requires effective cybersecurity. As the financial statements are officially disclosed, there is a risk of distortion or substitution of data. Stakeholders make management decisions on their financial interests and the operations of the economic entity based on reporting information. In order to discredit the company, its financial statements may be modified as a result of a cyber attack. Malicious actions of third parties may cause economic damage to the company at the time of accounting data transfer or at its storage location.

Disclosure of false information about the entity's activities may result in the loss of economic interest of stakeholders. In particular, investors may suspend further investment in the issuer's financial instruments; financial institutions may refuse lending; other creditors may demand early returns of accounts payable; contractors may refuse to cooperate, etc. As a result, an enterprise whose financial statements are distorted may suffer indirect financial damage that threatens economic security.

The level of communicative interaction between economic and cybersecurity of the enterprise is also connected with the communication with stakeholders. Cyberattacks at this level are aimed at blocking communications and transmitting false or incomplete accounting data to users. Stakeholders may consider such actions to be breaches of communication regulations or mistake the data altered by a cyber threat for the authentic information.

For example, if cyber threats target the company's communications with fiscal institutions, this may lead to false accounting information reaching the recipient. If the accounting data recorded in the enterprise's books as the tax base for accrued taxes (fees) and the data sent to the tax authority differ, this may result in financial sanctions. The tax agent then suffers economic losses from fines for failure to report, late or incomplete information sent to the fiscal authority about financial and economic activities. In the absence of effective cybersecurity of communications with regulatory institutions, threats to the economic security of the enterprise increase due to repeated penalties for violating fiscal regulations.

Direct cyber risks threaten banking communications. If the attackers gain access to the electronic transaction accounting system, they can steal funds from the bank and electronic accounts. The extent of economic damage from the manifestation of such cyber risks can be reliably determined. Unauthorized access to the system of accounting for non-cash payments threatens the economic security of the enterprise due to the possibility of losing all such funds. If the theft concerns electronic money or cryptocurrencies, it is impossible to search for attackers and recover lost funds. Given the confidentiality and impersonality of electronic transactions, effective preventive cybersecurity is crucial, as combating already active cyber threats is difficult.

Economic entities that use accounting and management outsourcing services are also vulnerable to significant economic losses. Active cyber threats can significantly modify accounting data in the process of communication from sender to outsourcer (Balaziuk et al., 2020). The outsourcing firm carries out further information processing on the basis of the received distorted data, which ultimately leads to them unwittingly creating false reports. The increased number of stages of accounting data processing, related to the transfer to the outsourcer, makes it very difficult to establish the reliability of accounting. Meanwhile, the repeated processing of newly credible accounting data after the elimination of cyber threats requires additional costs and time. Cyber threats related to outsourcing also increase the likelihood of losing confidential information due to the need for continuous electronic communications, which has the potential to cause economic damage to the company. Thus, the number of delegated accounting functions simultaneously affects the economic and the cybersecurity of the enterprise.

Communication with audit firms may be subject to similar cyber threats. If the auditor receives incomplete information about the financial and economic activities of the enterprise, they may choose to give a negative audit report or refuse to provide it at all. The use of such audit information may lead to a negative business reputation in the eyes of the auditor or other recipients of audit reports. A blow to business reputation has a negative impact on the economic security of the enterprise.

Should all cyber risks become reality, ultimately the business image of the enterprise is ruined, which determines the reputation level of the interaction between economic and cybersecurity. Hackers may inflict damage on an enterprise's reputation directly for the purpose of causing economic damage and suspending the operation of the economic entity, or indirectly while pursuing personal, in most cases financial, goals. In any case, the company subjected to cyberattacks loses confidence of employees, contractors, investors, creditors, public and state institutions. PR losses inevitably make a dent in the economic security of the enterprise.

Oversight and fiscal institutions, social and environmental organizations may impose financial sanctions, block the assets of the enterprise or consider its activities illegal. Information interaction with such business entities is considered “toxic”, which automatically hinders its financial and economic activities. Accounting stakeholders in such cases lose economic interest in the economic entity, suspend cooperation, postpone the fulfilment of contractual obligations, etc., which may cause insolvency, reduced liquidity and wavering financial stability of the enterprise.

The damage to the business image of the enterprise inevitably leads to the loss of its market value. The company’s securities are depreciated, the value of intangible assets decreases. Ultimately, the growing number and intensity of cyber threats reduces the company’s goodwill. More details on the impact of the quality of accounting information and the use of computer and communication technologies on the goodwill of an economic entity are offered in the research of (Zadorozhnyi et al., 2018).

The largest and most systematic cyberattacks can lead to a unique phenomenon – negative goodwill, when the market value of the company is lesser than the total fair value of its assets. Bankruptcy or reorganization of the enterprise is the final objectives of cyber threats aiming to damage the economic security. As a result, the reputation level covers all previous information levels of the interaction of economic and cybersecurity (Fig. 1.9).

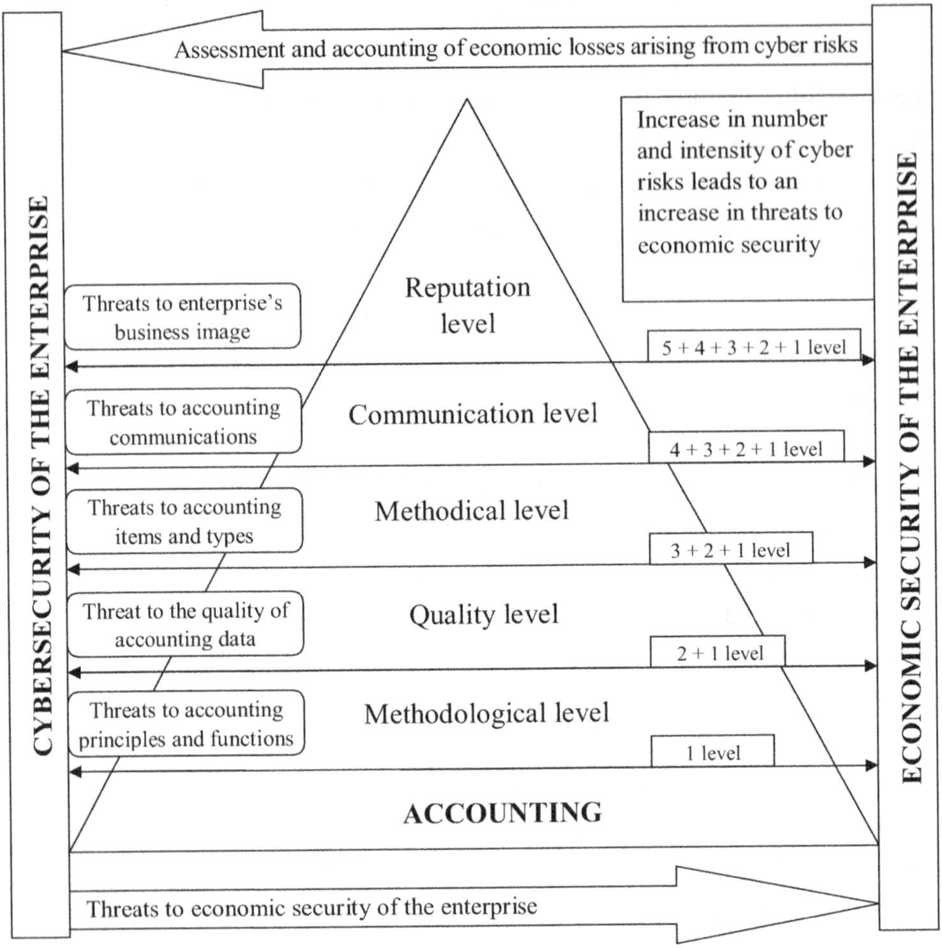

Fig. 1.9. Innovative multilevel accounting methodology for the interaction of economic and cybersecurity of enterprises

Source: created by the authors.

Each subsequent level of interaction of economic and cybersecurity of enterprises accumulatively covers the previous levels. The implementation of accounting techniques also shows the feedback between the economic security and cybersecurity of the enterprise. With the help of accounting methods for analysing economic processes, it is possible to reliably identify and assess losses from the manifestation of cyber risks. Economic losses from the growing number and intensity of cyber risks can differ significantly depending on the level of information interaction between economic and cybersecurity. The company incurs significant costs associated with the manifestation of cyber risks at the highest reputational level. These are difficult for accounting to identify and assess, and therefore require further research.

1.5. Classification of stakeholders (users) of accounting information for the enterprise cybersecurity purposes

Accounting forms an integrated information environment that connects the users of accounting information into a single system. Accounting professionals filling the system with information resources, and information agents (stakeholders) receive and use the resources for making management decisions. At each stage of accounting information processing at the internal and external levels of accounting and management interaction, the information environment of an enterprise is threatened by cyber threats.

Global hybrid conflicts, the COVID-19 pandemic, and the growing corruption of the economy have led to increased cyber risks in the field of accounting. Increasing in cyber-attacks as a part of hybrid wars involves manipulating, distorting, and replacing credentials to inflict economic damage for large enterprises and sectors of economy, ultimately damaging to the country's economic security. Pandemic changes in the work process distanced and isolated workers that required active information exchange between the workplaces of specialists and information base of enterprises. Active communication services using carry out functional responsibilities has attracted the attention of cybercriminals, whose goal is to steal trade secrets and intellectual property of the enterprise. Economic imbalances and corruption threats to businesses have a similar impact on accounting processes that leading to significant reductions in the business cybersecurity costs. As a result, the number of vulnerabilities in the cybersecurity system of accounting and management has increased significantly.

Therefore, the active development of computer and communication technologies in the digital economy has led to a variety of cyber threats due to the expansion of facilities and vulnerabilities in information system of enterprises. The variability of cyber risks directly depends on the type of stakeholders. Grouping users of credentials by different criteria for the cybersecurity purposes allows them to develop adequate methods to prevent, avoid and eliminate cyber-attacks more effectively.

The basic criterion for dividing users of accounting information into internal and external ones is the spatial location of stakeholders involved in the information environment of the enterprise. Internal staff and enterprise management of various levels are the main users of accounting information and moderators of management decisions, and are subject to frequent cyber-attacks consequently. As analyzed in the scholarly work (Chukhno, 2011), the scientists quite often consider information related only to the functioning of employees and owners (founders) of the enterprise as an object of cyber risk, so they recognizing the existence only internal users of accounting information in terms of the cybersecurity at enterprises. According to the EY Global Information Security Survey, personal information of employees, and information about owners and managers is the main object of cyber-attacks at enterprises (17% and 11%, respectively). In addition, 34% of businesses were exposed to active cyber threats due to negligence or ignorance of employees who are internal stakeholders (Table 1.4). In harmony to the EY Global Information Security Survey, most cyber-attacks (38%), are organized by current or fired employees (Is cybersecurity about more than protection, 2019).

Table 1.4

Objects and vulnerabilities of business cybersecurity

Object of a cyber-attacks	Fraction of enterprises	Cybersecurity's vulnerabilities	Fraction of enterprises
Staff's personal information	17 %	Negligent / uninformed employees	34 %
Information about financial and monetary transactions	12 %	Outdated security controls	26 %
Strategic plans	12 %	Unauthorized access by unauthorized persons	13 %
Information about owners and managers	11 %	Associated with using of cloud computing	10 %
Customer's information	11 %	Associated with smartphones / tablets	8 %
Research and development information	9 %	Related to social networks	5 %
Merger and acquisition information	8 %	Related with Internet of things	4 %
Intellectual property	6 %		
Supplier's information	5 %		

Source: based on (Is cybersecurity about more than protection, 2019).

However, accounting information, that related to external financial and economic processes, is being the object of cyber-attacks more often in the context of intensifying global hybrid conflicts and the COVID-19 pandemic (information about financial and monetary transactions – 12% of enterprises, information about customers – 11%, information about mergers and acquisitions– 8%, information about suppliers – 5%). 13% of businesses found that cyber threats became possible due to unauthorized access by persons, which are external to the information system of the enterprise (Is cybersecurity about more than protection, 2019). As a result, only the internal positioning of the cybersecurity is a limitation of its important mission in the formation of the comprehensive system of enterprise information and economic security.

At the same time, there are few scientific papers that significantly expand the users of accounting information in need of the cybersecurity. For example, N. L. Shishkova defined the list of ways of the cybersecurity in the context of separation on internal and external users. However, there is no explanation for the differences in providing cyber protection for different groups of stakeholders (Shyshko, 2016).

K. P. Borymskaya positions fiscal service as an important stakeholder of accounting information that is threatened by cyber-attacks. The scientist proposes the system of the cyber protection, that provides: definition of confidential information, improvement of job descriptions, using "digital signatures" for tax purposes, using software and hardware in the process of communication with fiscal service (Borymska, 2013). In return, A. Rasche and D. Esser developed information security standards separately for internal users and various external ones. According to scientists the users are recommended for using standards in obtaining and processing accounting information to protect it (Rasche and Esser, 2006). A similar opinion is held by C. Chikutuma, who justified the feasibility of forming integrated reporting as an effective communication channel for information transmission to both internal stakeholders and external ones. The researcher substantiates the demand for secure demarcation of information needs in different user groups to maintain trade secrets and ensure cyber protection of reporting entities (Chikutuma, 2016). The research was continued by V. A. Shpak with developing a method of protecting the document flow of the enterprise in the framework of information exchange with internal information contractors and external ones. The author substantiates the concept of confidential documents with different access rights to stakeholders (Shpak, 2015).

However, the differentiation of users according to the criterion of spatial location in relation to information environment of the enterprise makes it difficult to effectively ensure the cyber protection of enterprises due to the possibility of relating certain stakeholders to internal and external ones. It is difficult to develop tools for minimizing cyber threats when it is impossible to clearly cluster the subjects of security processes.

A large-scale study of scientific positions regarding to the options for classification of accounting information users was conducted by I. S. Chukhno. Based on the identified conflicts in the traditional classification of users on internal and external, the author proposes to proceed from the ability of stakeholders to manage the activities of the business entity. Accordingly, the researcher identified three groups of accounting information users:

1) persons, who make management decisions;

2) persons, who do not make management decisions, but have a financial interest;

3) persons without financial interest (Chukhno, 2012).

Sharing the opinion of scientist, it should be noted that the division of stakeholders on the basis of financial and managerial interest solves the problem of their association with internal persons or external ones. The staff together with the owners (founders), regardless of the spatial relationship to the information environment of the enterprise, can be both internal and external stakeholders.

O. A. Lagovska et al. were one of the first to classify stakeholders of accounting information for the cybersecurity purposes on users: with full right, with limited right and those who use freely published reporting (Bukhhalterskyi oblik v upravlinni pidpryiemstvom, 2017). A. Yu. Shchyrska has a similar position on separation of insiders and outsiders as accounting information users with the presence and absence of access rights to accounting information, respectively (Shchyrska, 2018).

Also Y. El-Ebiary and N. Alawi examining the risks of accounting as part of information system of the enterprise, determines the need to classify stakeholders according to the probability of cyber threats. Depending on the relevance of certain cyber threats for each three types of accounting information users (with high, medium and low probability), variable methods of the cybersecurity are needed (El-Ebiary and N. Alawi, 2020).

Hereby, the classical approaches to the classification of accounting information users are ineffective for the purposes of the enterprise cybersecurity. In other words, cyber threats may not change for stakeholders within a single classification group.

The main criterion for dividing users into groups for the purposes of the enterprise cybersecurity, to which these scientists pay attention, is the level of access to accounting information. The level of access should be interpreted as the maximum possible amount and type of credentials that are provided to users for processing, inasmuch their professional and behavioral characteristics. The right to receive accounting information under such conditions is directly related to the accessed possibility to trade secrets of the enterprise and derives from the accounting type (financial, management, etc.). According to this criterion, it is advisable to distinguish stakeholders with absolute access, full access, limited access and access to free information:

1) Users with absolute rights are management staff with unlimited access to accounting information used for long-term management of the enterprise. Such users embrace the maximum available array of data that generated by management and financial accounting.

2) Users with full rights have access to confidential information in a particular area of management, or financial and economic activities of the enterprise. For example, management personnel use management accounting credentials of a strategic or tactical nature to make strategic and tactical management decisions.

3) Users with limited access are provided with the right to implement subject-functional actions in relation to the enterprise, information on an individual aspect of that is provided for using. In particular, fiscal institutions receive tax reporting and request additional accounting

information in the form of primary and synthetic documents, etc. if it necessary.

4) Users with free access do not need a request to obtain the right for exploiting accounting information. They use publicly available data. Such accounting information does not contain confidential information and is mainly prepared by financial accounting.

If it possible, to dispose of the access right to accounting information, stakeholders should be classified into right providers (given the right to receive and dispose of data) and right holders (holders of information access rights). The users of information quite often can belong to both groups at the same time. The right holder on the rights of subcontracting may delegate (transfer the right of access) the authority to process information to other persons. For example, potential investors receive accounting information and passing it to investment brokers. Therefore, the right holder can be both the creditor.

Based on the implementation of the access right to accounting information, it is also advisable to distinguish the following classification criteria: access to accounting objects, functional rights and the order of information processing. According to the object direction, stakeholders are given the right to process information only about certain objects of accounting. For example, it is advisable to allow a cashier to work with the functional menu of computer programs for accounting and management of cash and banking transactions. Other objects of accounting remain inaccessible to the narrowly specialized specialist. The regulation of functional powers provides for the limited implementation of accounting functions: filling out primary documents, conducting control procedures, generalizing accounting data in registers, conducting tax calculations, etc. Depending on their job responsibilities, stakeholders may be prohibited from processing credentials, including: viewing or entering information; verify (conduct) data, change information that has taken effect; delete accounts; transfer indicators to the next stages of processing.

In accordance, the users of accounting information should be classified suitably to the following security criteria: functional rights (work with primary documents, control procedures (including inventory), systematization of data, analysis of indicators and decision-making; definition of accounting policy); processing of accounting information (entering, editing, conducting, summarizing, transmitting and archiving data); object of accounting (non-current assets, inventories, cash, receivables, accounts payable, capital, wages, taxes and fees, income and expenses or more detailed objects). Stakeholders are often endowed with combined rights. The smaller is the company, the greater is the concentration of user accounting information rights. In small businesses one person can perform all accounting processes, that involves obtaining full rights to operate information. Individual business entities that simultaneously perform economic, accounting and management functions, holders of absolute rights, as the right holder and the recipient is the one person.

The next classification feature of the stakeholders' division from standpoint of the need to provide the cybersecurity is the type of economic activity. Stakeholders that representing different types of economic activity are also exposed to variable cyber risks (Table 1.5). So, users of accounting information should be grouped by sector of the economy.

According to the research by the Union Agency for the cybersecurity in 2020 cyber threats to all economic activities have increased significantly, due to isolation, distancing, growth of information and financial resources to overcome the COVID-19 pandemic. Cyber risks for various sectors of economy could be completely different, for example for households – Fishing, Information Leakage, Data Theft, and for industry – Malware, Web AppAttacks, Insider Threat (unintentional abuse) (Sectoral thematic threat analysis ETL2020, 2020).

Table 1.5

Relevance of cyber threats for different sectors of economy

Sector	Maim threats	Trend in 2020 / 2019	Influence of factors
Individuals / Households	Fishing Information Leakage Data Theft	=	Self-isolation as a way to combat COVID-19 has contributed to the decentralization of the IT environment and the isolation of Internet users who are exposed to cyber threats and pay less attention to the cybersecurity.
Industry	Malicious Software (Malware) Web Application Attacks Insider Threat (unintentional abuse)	=	Theft of credentials containing trade secrets is a significant threat to this sector. Cyber-attacks on supply chains and industrial control systems are also a reason to suspend the production process
Multidisciplinary Business	Web Application Fishing Malicious Software	+	Workers' remote work as a way to combat COVID-19 has intensified Fishing attacks, threatening the loss of confidential credentials.
Public Administration, Defense, Social Services	Malicious Software Fishing Web Application Attacks	+	Using cloud services has led to an increase in cyber threats to the administrative sector of state. Social services were cyber-attacked through financial assistance services to citizens during the COVID-19 pandemic.
Finance / Banking Business / Insurance	Web App Attacks Insider Threat (unintentional abuse) Malicious Software Data Theft	=	The multifaceted nature of the financial sector in economy makes it difficult to clearly identify cyber threats, as different areas of financial and banking services may be exposed to completely different cyber risks in the field of accounting.
Healthcare / Medicine	Malicious Software Insider Threat (unintentional abuse) Web App Attacks	+	Cyber threats to health care have become more relevant due to the interest of fraudsters in the information and financial resources allocated to the fight against the COVID-19 pandemic.
Education	Malicious Software Demanding Program Web App Attacks	+	Increasing the activity of cyber espionage campaigns due to the interest in accounting and scientific resources related to the COVID-19 study.
Information and Communication	Web App Attacks Insider Threat (unintentional abuse) Malicious Software	=	As the number of digital media grows, cyber risks of changing public information to control public opinion become relevant.
Arts, Entertainment and Games	Web App Attacks Malicious Software Fishing	=	The transition from licensing to subscription sales of intellectual works for gaming industry via the Internet has made this sector more attractive to cybercriminals.

Source: systematized on the basis of (Sectoral thematic threat analysis ETL2020, 2020).

The type of actual cyber threats for each sector of economy also depends on the affiliation of stakeholders to individuals or legal entities. When dividing accounting information users into individuals and legal entities, it is necessary to take into account age parameters, organizational and legal form, respectively. Differentiated cyber threats are inherent in individuals of a certain age. Diverse age groups of stakeholders are characterized by special behavioral characteristics, that increase the impact of certain cyber risks. According to the age structure of stakeholders, it is advisable to rank them into groups: junior (up to 35 years old), middle (36-50 years old), senior (51-65 years old) and elderly (over 66 years old).

Younger users mainly receive information through social networks and messengers that requires limited use of them for business and management purposes. The middle age group is the most active among other stakeholders in using software to handle accounting information, as well as specialized in Internet pages. Such people are mostly at risk of virus and hacker attacks, which requires using anti-virus programs. Older stakeholders are more likely to be attacked by Fishing and Spam attacks via e-mail, as well as using payment services and bank cards. It is advisable to use firewalls, spam filters and additional verification systems for electronic transactions. Elderly users are more susceptible to fraudulent use of telephones (calls and messages), which requires the use of specialized software to filter telephone traffic.

It is clearly the isolation of cyber threats for each age group is conditional, but these risks are the most likely and typical for the relevant stakeholders at the same time. Due to the influence of age and behavioral characteristics users of accounting information are protected from some cyber risks and susceptible to others.

In the contrast to the age structuring of individuals, it is advisable for legal entities to apply the classification according to their organizational and legal form. In order to strengthen the cybersecurity of legal entities, it is expedient to divide into: joint-stock companies (use and be sure to disclose large amounts of accounting information in accordance with law), companies (limited liability to counterparties), government agencies and institutions containing confidential information containing state secret), associations of enterprises (using a system of complex permanent communications between members of the association), non-entrepreneurial entities (have a significant informational impact on the social, cultural, domestic, religious functioning of society).

Each group of business entities has different features of processing accounting information. Depending on the type of organizational and legal form, cyber threats are also different. For example, state institutions are subject to significant hacking attacks in order to steal state secret or harm national security. The separation of these groups makes it possible to identify the most likely cyber risks and develop preventive measures to ensure the cybersecurity.

An important criterion for classifying stakeholders is the type of communication channels used in terms of access to accounting information. Most modern business communications are implemented over the Internet. Accordingly, users (senders, recipients) of accounting information should be divided into persons who appliance: e-mail (various e-mail services), data exchange algorithms between accounting software products (eg, data synchronization 1C: Accounting and MEDoc), social networks and messengers (Facebook, VK, Viber, Whatsapp, Telegram, etc.), file sharing and cloud storage (Dropbox, OneDrive, Google Drive, etc.), internal data network (local area network), physical media (paper documents, flash media, CDs).

The complexity of control actions depends on the type of communication channel that traditionally used by stakeholders. Users of accounting information who exploit several channels of transmission (receipt) of information are exposed to more complex and frequent cyber risks. Information operations of some stakeholders, such as those using social networks and messengers, require permanent cybersecurity. Conversely, users of information on physical media are almost not exposed to cyber risks.

The classification of stakeholders by type of communication channels should also be used to restrict access to certain Internet services in the process of implementing functional responsibilities to prevent cyber threats. Additionally, there may be a nationwide ban for using Internet resources that could threaten country's cybersecurity. For example, in Ukraine, access to social networks VK, Odnoklasniki, mail.ru, file sharing and search engine Yandex, accounting software 1C: Accounting and many others, using which leads to the potential loss of information that containing trade and military secrets.

Besides the type of communication channel, the frequency of information acts is important for the cybersecurity. Depending on the frequency of requests or receipt of credentials, the likelihood of cyber threats increases. Therefore, it is advisable to separate stakeholders, to assess the necessary cybersecurity measures, from: permanent (synchronization of information occurs on a regular basis), frequent (daily information exchange), periodic (transmission and receipt of information occurs at certain intervals: every week, end of month or quarter, etc.) and single communications (after the need for accounting information, for example, the investor once a year to search for investment objects).

The generalized classification of accounting information users is shown in Table 1.6 by criteria: the ability to manage the activities of the business entity, the right of access, the likelihood of cyber threats, the ability to dispose of the right of access, access to accounting objects, functional law, information processing, economic activity, age of individuals, organizational and legal form legal entities, type of communication channels used, frequency of information acts.

Table 1.6

Classification of accounting information stakeholders in order to ensure the cybersecurity of enterprises

№	Classification criterion	Type of stakeholder
1.	Type of economic activity	Individuals / Households; Industry; Diversified Business; Public Administration, Defense, Social Services; Finance / Banking Business / Insurance; Healthcare / Medicine; Education; Information and Communication; Arts, Entertainment and Games
2.	Ability to manage the activities of the business entity	Persons who make management decisions; persons who do not do management decisions, but have a financial interest; persons without financial interest
3.	The right to access accounting information	With absolute rights; with full rights; with limited access; with free access
4.	The probability of cyber threats	With a high probability; with a medium probability; with a low probability
5.	Ability to dispose of the right of access	Right provider; right recipient
6.	Access to account objects	With the right to access information about: non-current assets; stocks; cash; receivables; payables; capital; salary; taxes and fees; income and expenses; more detailed objects
7.	Functional law	With the right to: work with primary documents; carrying out control procedures; data systematization; analysis of indicators and decision-making; definition of accounting policies
8.	The order of information processing	With the right to: data entry; data editing; data management, data generalization, data transfer and archiving
9.	Age of an individual	Younger age group; middle age group; senior age group; elderly age group
10.	Organizational and legal form of a juristic entity	Corporations; business associations; government agencies and institutions; business associations; on-entrepreneurial entities
11.	Type of used communication channels	What to use: email; algorithms for data exchange between accounting software products; social networks and messengers; file sharers and cloud storage; internal data network; physical media
12.	Frequency of information acts	With permanent; with frequent; with periodic; with singles

Source: developed by the author.

Except for the proposed options for the division of stakeholders, the company's management can independently add to the list of arbitrary types of accounting information users that will meet security needs. Instead some classification criteria, such as the number of full-time employees or the amount of profit, that are decisive in identifying different types of entities, do not affect the likelihood of cyber risks.

In the conditions of digital economy formation, economic entities carry out economic activity with minimal involvement of human resources. Information and economic processes in e-business enterprises are largely automated, and, therefore, the number of employees does not affect the manifestation of cyber threats and business profitability. The amount of profit also does not determine the likelihood of cyber threats. The need for the cybersecurity is similar for commercial, state, municipal or public institutions. Therefore, a separate classification of stakeholders by level of profitability is impractical for the organization of information security. Similarly, other criteria traditionally used to classify businesses are not relevant for the purposes of the cybersecurity at enterprises that requires further scientific substantiation and research.

CHAPTER 2. IMPROVING ACCOUNTING METHODS FOR THE PURPOSES OF CYBERSECURITY OF ENTERPRISES

2.1. Documentation and document flow based on blockchane technology for cybersecurity of the accounting system

In order to ensure cybersecurity, business management, regardless of the size of the business, resorts to isolating confidential information from other information flows. Corporate associations create a separate confidential document management service. For this purpose, use specialized software for processing, movement and storage of confidential documents isolated from the general document management system. Employees who handle information containing trade secrets are prohibited from using media and the Internet for personal purposes in the workplace. Temporal and semantic regulations of information processing are introduced. In particular, it regulates the time of access and content of information, access to which must be limited.

In addition to the above approaches to cybersecurity of information, document management is protected, as proved by V.A. Shpak, based on the implementation of additional rules:

- personal responsibility of employees for the preservation of the media and the secrecy of information;
- restriction of business necessity of access of personnel to documents, cases and databases;
- strict regulation of the procedure for working with documents, files and databases for all categories of staff (Shpak, 2015).

However, the isolation approach to documentation and document management does not guarantee effective cybersecurity of the enterprise. Separate credential databases are attracting the attention of cybercriminals. There is also always an insider influence on cybersecurity, which is realized through the possible recruitment of employees by third parties.

Insiders with access to confidential information may pass it on to cybercriminals. Another option is to secretly embed malicious software in the system of confidential document management for the purpose of information espionage by regular officials. As a result, there are cyber threats to the isolated information flows of enterprises. Therefore, to ensure effective cybersecurity, it is necessary to study new formats of documentation and document management.

Scientists have studied various aspects of the use of blockchain technology in accounting. For example, S.K. Bansal et al (2018) investigated promising trends in accounting development; D.E. O'Leary (2017) - technology architecture with the definition of flows of accounting information; S.M. Rındasu (2019) - benefits and threats to accounting; C.W. Cai (2021) - the ability to implement a triple account; J.G. Coyne and P.L. McMickle (2017) - overcoming organizational barriers to accounting; S. Sarkar (2018) - transformation of knowledge, skills and professional skills of accounting professionals; M. Karajovic et al. (2019) - a new way of structuring accounting information; M.D. Sheldon (2018) and S. Sinha (2020) - threats to the accounting profesion; J. Kokina et al. (2017) - threats to the accounting system.

There are also studies on the use of blockchain technology to improve information systems that are informationally related to accounting: J. Schmitz and G. Leoni (2019) - prospects for the development of audit and other types of control; S. Kozlowski (2018) - permanent audit with the formation of the control ecosystem of the enterprise; M. Liu et al. (2019) - synergetic relationship of accounting and auditing; A.A. Gomaa et al. (2019) - implementation of ERP systems and the role of accounting information in enterprise management; B.S. Tan and K.Y. Low (2019) - formation of databases for the purposes of different user groups; J. Wu et al. (2019) - the relationship with other types of computer and communication technology for variable information users and other scientists.

In the scientific space there are generalizing and review works concerning the application of blockchain technology in accounting. In particular, Erica Pimentel and Emilio Bouliann identified seven main areas of implementation of blockchain structuring of accounting information: the future of accounting, accounting functions, audit and control procedures, the display of cryptocurrencies in enterprise reporting, training of accounting professionals, administrative management, taxation. Scientists summarize the need to establish parity between theoretical research and practical developments on the implementation of blockchain technology in accounting (Pimentel and Bouliann, 2020).

Hashim Zeyad Alsaqa et al. concluded that the use of blockchain technology radically changes the accounting information system in the enterprise. In other words, the use of the principles of chain-block structuring of accounting information is impossible in the traditional accounting system, and requires a radical improvement of methodology, methodology and organization of accounting (Alsaqa et al., 2020).

Adriana Tiron Tudor et al. explored the main obstacles to the introduction of blockchain technology in accounting and auditing organizations. Scientists have identified the unwillingness of enterprises to innovate as the main organizational constraint on the use of innovative technologies and formed a method of SWOT-analysis of the use of blockchain technology for various accounting and auditing organizations. There are also seven promising areas of research on the implementation of blockchain technology in accounting practice: ensuring information transparency and accessibility; formation of start-up contracts between participants of contractual relations; participation of accounting specialists in the formation of the blockchain ecosystem; optimization of daily operation of accounting staff; providing training and retraining on activities with innovative technologies; transformation of accounting and auditing professions; institutional changes and improvements of regulatory and legal support (Tiron Tudor, 2021).

Intensification of scientific research on the peculiarities of the use of blockchain technology for accounting purposes took place in 2018. The most relevant research on the implementation of accounting and auditing functions in terms of block-chain structuring of information. The problem of formation of primary and reporting documents and training and retraining of accounting specialists in the conditions of implementation of the newest computer and communication technologies has appeared as unpopular research objects. The peak of activity in the formation of global scientific thought on the accounting aspect of the implementation of blockchain technology was in 2021, due to significant public attention to cryptographic assets (Fig. 2.1).

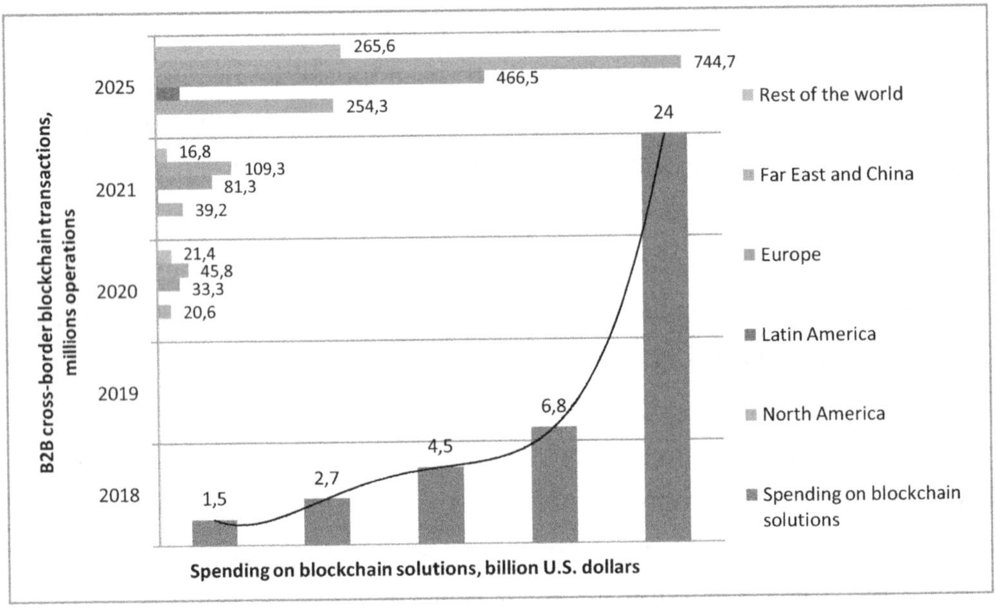

Fig. 2.1. Popularization of blockchain technology in 2018-2025

Source: formed on the basis of (Worldwide spending on blockchain solutions from 2017 to 2025; B2B cross-border transactions on blockchain in various regions worldwide in 2020 with forecasts from 2021 to 2025)

Investment in blockchain technology is expected to increase from $ 4.5 billion to $ 6.8 billion in 2021, and will reach $ 24 billion in 2025. The number of information operations using the principles of block-chain structuring of information is increasing in each of the geographical regions. The leaders in the introduction of blockchain technology are the countries of the Far East and China and Europe, which is confirmed by the nationality of researchers in the field of blockchain structuring of information.

However, scientists in the field of accounting and related research and application areas have paid inadequate attention to the possibilities of using blockchain technology to ensure cybersecurity of accounting information.

Summarizing the work of scientists in the field of blockchain technology, it is possible to systematize its fundamental principles for positioning the possibility of cybersecurity of information in Table. 2.1.

In the scientific search for prospects for cybersecurity of enterprises based on the use of blockchain technology in accounting, it is necessary to focus on its fundamental principles: fragmentation, complementarity, scalability, duplication, chronology, confidentiality, distribution, accessibility, openness of accounting information processing.

Most of the documents in the information cycle of enterprises are of accounting origin. Accounting generates primary economic information. Documentation of economic processes and phenomena is a primary element of the method of accounting. Therefore, economic data collected and documented are called "primary". Primary documentation is the initial stage of processing accounting information. Cybersecurity of the entire information system of the enterprise depends on the reliability and reliability of the information contained in the primary documents.

Cyber threats to paper documentation and document management have traditionally been positioned as internal malicious manipulation of employees or accidental errors.

Table 2.1

Principles of blockchain technology in terms of cybersecurity of accounting information

№	Fundamental principle	Implementation for purposes cybersecurity accounting information
1.	Fragmentation	Division of accounting information into separate fragments (blocks), which separately have no value for cyber attackers
2.	Mutual complement	Each block complements other blocks of information through a chain combination. When creating a new block, data about it is entered into all other related blocks, which prevents the fictitious appearance of new credentials
3.	Scalability	New blocks and modules can be added to the database without restrictions, which facilitates the use of unified cybersecurity systems for accounting information in all enterprises, regardless of business size, legal form or other organizational factors.
4.	Duplication	Each block can be duplicated in other storage locations, allowing you to recover accidentally lost or destroyed credentials
5.	Chronology	A chronological list of changes in accounting information is maintained, which allows to detect unauthorized actions that led to deviations from the reference sample
6.	Confidentiality	All accounting information processing operations are performed outside of official or government services, which makes it impossible to control and track the actions of accounting or management professionals.
7.	Distribution	Accounting information is placed in a distributed database, in which each of the fragments can be stored on many directly unrelated technical devices that are not owned by the enterprise. Cyber threats to software and hardware are impossible.
8.	Accessibility	Credentials are stored in public cloud databases, which prevents cybercriminals from blocking access
9.	Openness	The technology is open to use, making it popular in the financial, commercial, fiscal, administrative and, most importantly, security sectors.

Source: systemized and improved by the author.

Another source of external receipt of unreliable documents are the company's counterparties, which may change the credentials for a certain economic gain. Instead, in the conditions of transition to electronic documentation and document circulation, external cyber threats of the enterprise become more active. Primary credentials become a valuable information resource and, accordingly, the object of cyberattacks.

In traditional document management with elements of isolation of accounting information, it is mandatory to regulate the path of the document from sender to recipient. Potential recipients of credentials generate information requests and send them to the database. From the general information array is a selection of indicators that are useful and necessary for a particular type of stakeholders. Restricting access to confidential documents is important to ensure cybersecurity. Dosing of accounting information takes place through a system of filters that select and block documents on the way to the recipient. That is, the stakeholder receives information in accordance with information requests and access rights. The initiator of the information process in terms of traditional document management at the enterprise are users of accounting information, which is detrimental to the timeliness and security of accounting.

Instead, the organization of document flow based on blockchain technology minimizes the need to regulate information flows. The fact of occurrence of a financial and economic phenomenon or event and its reflection in the primary documents triggers a further information process. Based on the study of information preferences of stakeholders, identification of the right of access to trade secrets, job descriptions, an automated management system is able to cluster and distribute information. The documented array of credentials at the time of its occurrence and fixation in the accounting system can be automatically sent to the target user.

Accounting information is promptly received by the stakeholder, who is responsible for its processing or requires a full information resource for timely management decisions. The time criteria for processing accounting information are optimized. Unlike traditional document management, documented data with a small time lag is transmitted simultaneously for further processing or consumption. In the system of electronic document management, it is advisable to provide a method of controlling the feedback to the accounting information received by stakeholders. It is necessary to control the fact that the user receives primary data, their processing by officials, the availability of appropriate management decisions to adjust the activities of the business entity, etc. Errors are impossible when controlling feedback; information duplication;

With blockchain technology, accounting information is fragmented into numerous components, which can be duplicated with the accumulation in different blocks and supplemented for future integration into a single set. Each piece of information can be stored on various technical devices or cloud information processing services. With the use of blockchain structuring information, the need for additional means of cybersecurity of the enterprise disappears.

Enterprise cybersecurity based on blockchain technology is implemented through fragmentation and random distribution of accounting information immediately at the time of its documentation. After collection, the primary data are broken down into separate information arrays, directly unrelated to each other. Additionally, it is possible to encrypt information and write to a distributed cloud environment. Each piece of credentials does not carry a semantic load. Only the end user integrates the elements of accounting information into a single information model, which can be useful and valuable for further use. Fragmented credentials can be open because without further aggregation it has no informational value for cybercriminals. The need for the organization of isolated document management systems decreases,

Through the use of blockchain technology, reliable security protection of business communications is implemented. Documentary support of business relationships requires effective cyber defense in order to prevent the manifestation of cyber threats. Documents entered by the counterparty must be fragmented and encrypted when entered into a single database. Contractual relations contracted in the documents are protected from third-party changes. Unconditional changes by the parties to the business relationship are also impossible. It is expedient to control the fulfillment of contractual obligations on the basis of monitoring of primary documents on realization of material values (works, services) and monetary transactions.

To implement cyber protection of accounting information between counterparties by mutual agreement, it is advisable to use a single cloud document management service. In other words, all parties to the contractual relationship choose the Internet platform for joint paperwork for the execution and execution of commercial agreements. It is advisable to integrate cloud document management services into the internal information systems of enterprises. As a result, the original design or incoming receipt of electronic copies of documents are recorded simultaneously in two databases: each company and the information association of contracting companies. Promising in the context of the digital economy is also the information integration of all counterparties into a single database of electronic document management based on blockchain technology.

Blockchain technology detects arrays of information that have been the object of internal or external cyberattacks. For example, on the basis of monitoring the history of changes in certain documents and comparing them with reference samples, it is advisable to identify persons - violators of the information regime. Instead, the fact of the appearance of unauthorized external changes in the information environment of the enterprise, which differ from similar information arrays from other sources, may be evidence of cyber intervention. The detected incident, which took place in violation of the time, information and legal regulations, should be regarded as a cyberattack. In case of loss, distortion or destruction of information fragments by attackers, their automatic recovery from the distributed database is possible.

Chain-block structuring of accounting information simplifies the process of archival storage of documents. The distributed database of credentials should be placed in a network of interconnected cloud services, which ensures the availability of archival information for users. Cloud archiving of electronic documents on a network of interconnected servers guarantees their storage, round-the-clock access and cybersecurity. At the request of stakeholders, disparate arrays of archival accounting information are removed from electronic archives and recombined to display the document in the traditional form as a set of certain details. Such stakeholders can be both internal users of information (accounting or management specialists) and external - controlling or fiscal institutions.

To access electronic documents, a system of digital signatures is used, which is already actively used for fiscal purposes and to obtain various government administrative services. The use of electronic keys should take place in two stages: the formation of primary documents and their recovery from a distributed database. After collecting the credentials, it is advisable to digitally sign the persons responsible for the formation of primary documents, which provides control of information authorship. Then there is the fragmentation and encryption of accounting information, which after reaching the target consumer is recombined to the original form. To gain access, the user of the recovered information also uses a personalized digital signature, which is evidence of the fact of information processing or consumption.

It is advisable to restrict the access rights of stakeholders to the credential database by setting the validity period of electronic keys. The need to organize cybersecurity encourages frequent changes in the digital signature of staff. The need to reissue digital signatures encourages stakeholders to update security discipline. Each user is forced to apply to the issuer for a new electronic key, which facilitates permanent control and verification of stakeholders. The company's management has an effective method of controlling the legality of the use of electronic formats for verification of a person trying to gain access to confidential information.

Through the use of electronic key systems, users gain access to the dosed amount of information within the open document flow. The proposed information scheme of open document management based on blockchain technology is shown in Fig. 2.2.

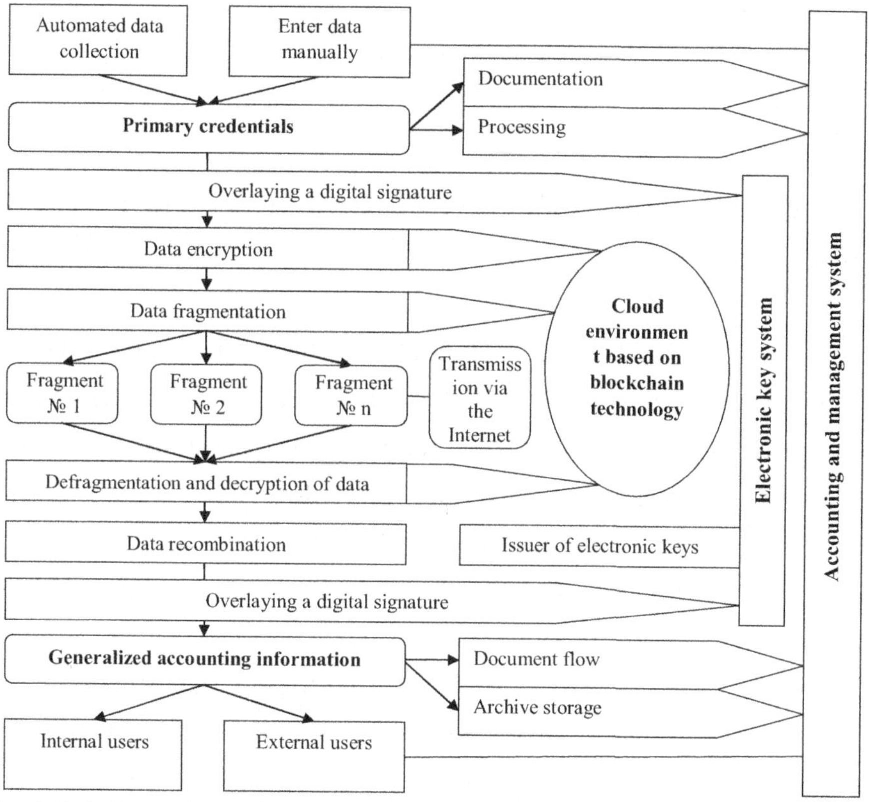

Fig. 2.2. Information scheme of open document flow based on blockchain technology

Source: developed by the author.

Implementation of electronic documentation and document management based on the principles of data openness using blockchain technology is the main organization of cybersecurity in all enterprises, regardless of ownership, business size, etc. The rejection of isolation practices in the organization of information exchange in the business environment of enterprises is an element of the formation of an open national economy. The circulation of accounting information in terms of effective cybersecurity at the internal and external levels is an incentive for further development of new technologies in the financial and economic sphere ("fintech industry").

2.2. Accounting and cybersecurity of electronic transactions using cryptocurrencies

The progressive development of electronic money has led to the emergence of digital cash, where its active use is associated with an increase in the volume of electronic transactions for goods (work, services), implemented through the Internet. The latest trend in the development of the technology of electronic transactions is the emergence of cryptocurrency, the turnover of which takes place through telecommunication links between taxpayers' personal electronic wallets to recipients of funds (Yak pysaty i vymovliaty bitcoin, 2021).

The technology of cryptocurrencies is based on the blockchain communication system, which is a union of public registers for accumulation of information on money transactions. The integrity of the blockchain is implemented through the duplication of the entire amount of information in other user of the electronic payment system. In other words, there is no shared data warehouse, no single server, which accumulates all the information. Therefore, the lost part of the information in one digital cash holder is offset by other owners of electronic wallets.

Such features of the cryptocurrencies as complete confidentiality and lack of centralized control by state and a single issuer, distinctly differs them from other electronic payment systems. These characteristics contribute to the use of cryptocurrencies by offenders in cyberattacks. Cryptocurrency is accepted by extortionist programs and cyberterrorists. With the help of cryptocurrencies is the legalization of funds obtained by criminal means. Therefore, the use of cryptocurrencies as a new confidential type of electronic money will inevitably be accompanied by cyber risks. Activation of cyberthreats in the field of cryptocurrency circulation can be demonstrated by the statistical data (Fig. 2.3).

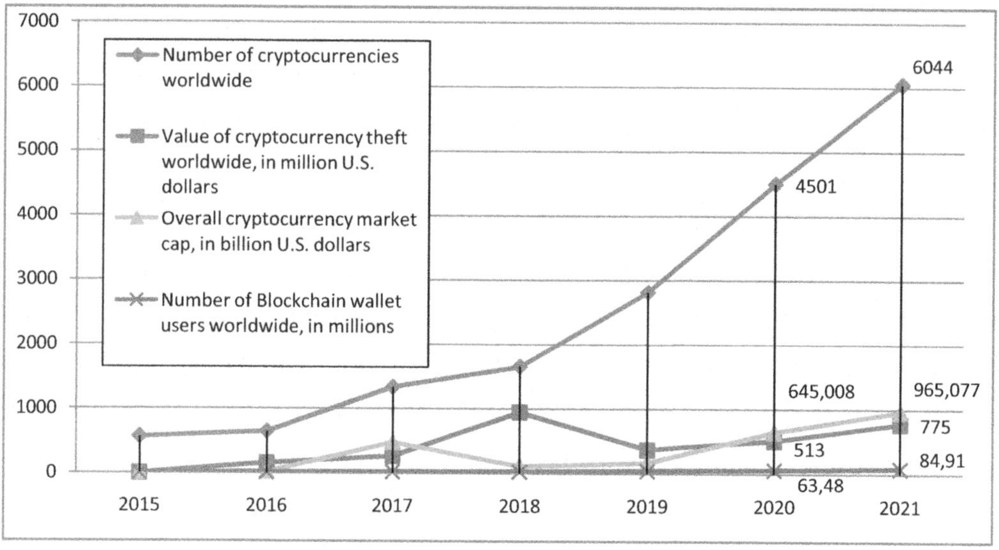

Fig. 2.3. Trends in the cryptocurrency market

Source: (Number of cryptocurrencies worldwide from 2013 to 2021; Value of cryptocurrency theft worldwide from 2016 to 2020; Estimate of overall cryptocurrency market cap per week from July 2010 to June 2021; Number of Blockchain wallet users worldwide)

The number of types of cryptocurrencies increases significantly every year on a global scale. Since 2016 along with the growth of the cryptocurrencies market capitalization the number of thefts and other cyber threats in the field of cryptocurrency circulation has been increasing. In 2021 value of cyber fraud is estimated at $ 965 million. And in 2018 this indicator peaked at almost $ 1 billion.

The number of scientists whose scientific subject and applied research are cryptocurrencies is increasing with the growth of cryptocurrency circulation. However, scientific proposals have been formed by the authors in the majority of cases according to the formal signs of cryptocurrencies and related to the elimination of shortcomings in the use of cryptocurrencies. It is necessary to carry out a comprehensive study of the accounting and cybersecurity of electronic transactions with the allocation of cryptocurrency as a separate object, which radically changes the process of electronic settlements and is a factor in ensuring the enterprises cybersecurity.

The cryptocurrency exchanges and cash transaction systems are functioning based on the use of electronic communication channels for transfer of accounting data. Applying the “Internet Bank” and “Client-Bank” systems, which use communication relations to provide information about the status of an account and authorization to execute transactions, are the current trends in ensuring the management of cashless settlements. The main differences between the two systems are the need to use special software (“Client-Bank”) and / or web page with access to the Internet (“Internet Bank”) for the exchange of information.

The downside to banking via the Internet is a functional limitation of such an option of account management due to the preservation of all the accounting information in a banking institution and a possibility of working only in on-line mode. Internet banking is mainly used by individuals and legal entities with insignificant money turnover, which require periodic information on the status of an account. As such, information from the “Internet Bank” system cannot be used for further implementation of control and accounting procedures due to its incompatibility with the software of enterprises.

Internet banking is threatened by active cyber risks associated with the Internet functioning. First of all, attackers can block access to the global network through public communication channels. Attackers create clones of Internet banking sites. Such sites intercept information to obtain personalized data used to access bank accounts. Data is monitored through the parallel forwarding of all money transactions to third-party servers. In the future, such data are used by offenders to steal money from bank accounts. It is possible to view the history of money transactions to establish the amount and recipients (senders) of non-cash payments, which allows attackers to identify the company's counterparties and compliance with payment discipline. Therefore, the exchange of information through the communication channel "Internet Bank" is unreliable from the cybersecurity.

Slightly greater cybersecurity of credentials is provided by banking communications "Client-Bank". Modern software products for the accounting automation support the “Client-Bank” system for downloading bank account statements and sending payment documents in electronic form. However, the universal software is not able to take into account the individual features of communication technologies of different banking institutions and issuers of electronic money, which makes it impossible to use them freely. Also, the disadvantages of the “Client-Bank” system are the following: lack of ownership of the software installed in a workplace of an accountant; possible incompatibility of the software of the “Client-Bank” with other software systems at an enterprise; lack of mobility of the system usage (the software is installed on one or two computers of accounting staff, which creates restrictions on the system use through mobile devices and gadgets); need for presence of all persons, who must sign a payment document in one place with personal computers, on which the software is installed; significant expenses for installing the necessary software of the remote banking system and further maintenance by a banking institution (Honcharuk, 2012).

The threat to the operation of software on the principles of "Client-Bank" technology is the introduction of malicious Trojan viruses into the program code. Infection can occur at the time of software update, connection to the database of the banking (financial) institution. If the «Client-Bank» software database is stored not on cloud or virtual servers, but in the local network of the enterprise, there is a possibility of loss (damage) of accounting information.

Also attackers using periodic (sometimes once a day) synchronization of data between the software "Client-Bank" and the database of the banking (financial) institution are able to distort the accounting indicators about funds to misinform the management. The use of inaccurate accounting information can lead to error transfers of funds to third parties or wrong management decisions.

A new type of cyber threat associated with the use of malicious software is cryptojacking (illegal mining). Covert cryptocurrency mining is a type of cyber attack due to the illegal use of hardware and software without the consent of the owners. Banking, and especially other financial institutions, by distributing user software "Client-Bank", can use it for cryptojacking. Illegal mining is difficult to detect, so it is best to avoid software installations from unknown financial institutions.

Therefore, the communication technologies "Internet Bank" and "Client-Bank" cannot be effective for ensuring cybersecurity and organization of information exchange between cryptocurrency circulation systems and their accounting at the enterprise. The phenomenon of cryptocurrencies is based on the blockchain technology, the implementation of which involves uniting all the owners of electronic money through a network of communication channels, which does not require the existence of a single centre for processing and accumulation of data.

The combination of functional advantages of the blockchain technology and the positive qualities of the “Internet-Bank” and “Client-Bank” communications will allow to create a hybrid system of non-cash payments with the cryptocurrencies, electronic money, money on bank accounts through payment cards and the effective cyber defense of information exchange with all the participants in settlement operations (hereinafter - the hybrid system). It is advisable to organize a hybrid system on the basis of blockchain technology, which allows avoiding many cyber risks inherent in banking communications "Internet Bank" and "Client Bank".

Functioning of a hybrid system involves publishing of a software source code for public familiarization. Similarly for all electronic money, it is necessary to provide free access to the universal software module for non-cash settlements. Many e-money issuers already provide free applications on the "Internet Banking" that can be embedded in a web page for payment acceptance. Buyers gain a convenient mechanism of non-cash settlements for goods and services purchased through the Internet. Hybridization is also realized thanks to the free convertibility of all the existing monetary funds. Any cryptocurrency can be purchased for electronic money or funds on bank accounts. The process is also reverse, receiving digital cash from a payer provides for the possibility of its transfer to a bank account and cash withdrawal from an ATM network.

However, the integration of payment systems on the principles of blockchain technology should also be carried out in the direction of providing the information on cash transactions in accounting software to provide cybersecurity. Developers of computer programs for accounting automation will be able to embed a hybrid system into software of universal or individual application. Due to the information integration of electronic payment system into accounting software, the problem of recognizing ownership of a computer program is solved, and the information incompatibility in the organization of an enterprise management is completely eliminated. Automation of accounting of non-cash transactions takes place in combination with other areas of accounting work in a single software complex. It is recommended to place a hybrid system into the foundation of the automated accounting of funds with access to non-cash transactions to the persons responsible, with provision of remoteness in the management of funds, with organization of effective cybersecurity and control on the part of management of an enterprise and community regarding the expediency of monetary transactions, etc.

Thanks to the hybrid system, the main disadvantage of the Client-Bank communication technology is solved, which is incidental to the inability to use the program at many workstations of accounting and management specialists. All employees of an enterprise, whose activities are related to money transactions, it is recommended to provide access to the account information on the receipt of funds to a current account. For example, in places of supply of goods, it is useful for employees to have information about the previous receipt of funds from a buyer, which will allow to initiate the issuance of an order. Separation of access to the system of money transactions and accounting information should be carried out on the basis of personal digital signatures (logins and passwords) depending on the positioning of the employee in the hierarchical management structure.

More generalized data is recommended to provide managers of various hierarchical levels with Internet access and allow manipulations through a web-based browser from an arbitrary workplace. There is an integration of the advantages of the systems "Internet Bank" and "Client-Bank" for the automated execution of control and accounting procedures over information about the status and changes in the balance of funds. Being territorially distant from an enterprise or place of transfer's execution, a manager and an accountant will be able to monitor the process of executing a transaction through a personal mobile device. Also, it is expedient to preliminary assign the implementation of licensing functions for payment execution to the managers of different hierarchical levels. At the moment of initiating a non-cash transfer, a relevant manager will be notified of payment options and permission or prohibition of a transaction. It is advisable in the accounting policy of an enterprise to indicate the monetary threshold, the achievement of which requires a sanction of accounting and managerial staff. If the limit is not exceeded, then there is no request. To the contrary, in the case of a non-cash transaction for an over-limit amount, there is a need for a multiple authorization from several accounting and management specialists. This way, the cybersecurity of money transactions is realized and personalization of the responsibility for monetary transactions is ensured.

Using a hybrid system eliminates the procedure of drawing up a paper primary document. It is not always possible to form a primary settlement document in a traditional, typical form. Given the confidentiality of cryptocurrencies, it is difficult to identify a payer, which prevents filling the basic details of any original document. Only a code of a monetary transaction, which certifies the repayment of the related debt, is indicated in the automated accounting system. In our opinion, the role of a traditional bank statement, on the basis of which the account holdings were formed, is significantly reduced in the accounting in case of electronic transfers. All primary information about the movement of electronic money and cryptocurrencies for a certain period goes to an accountant, who has the opportunity to monitoring, in an expeditious manner, the remaining balances of accounts.

On the basis of electronic primary information about crediting of funds to an enterprise's account, which go into an accounting department in an automatic mode without delay, the further accounting procedures can be automated. It is assumed that when a product buyer or customer authorizes transferring of electronic money or cryptocurrencies from a personal electronic wallet, the business operations and the formation of accounting records is automatically included in the accounting system. Similarly for the recipient, entry of information though the hybrid system on receipt of non-cash funds to an electronic wallet initiates the automatic formation of corresponding record on the financial accounts in software. The scheme of information flows in the conditions of automated accounting and control of funds on the basis of applying the hybrid system of payment operations with electronic money, cryptocurrencies, funds on bank accounts with integration of the functions of the "Internet Bank" and "Client-Bank" blockchain technologies, are shown in Fig. 2.4.

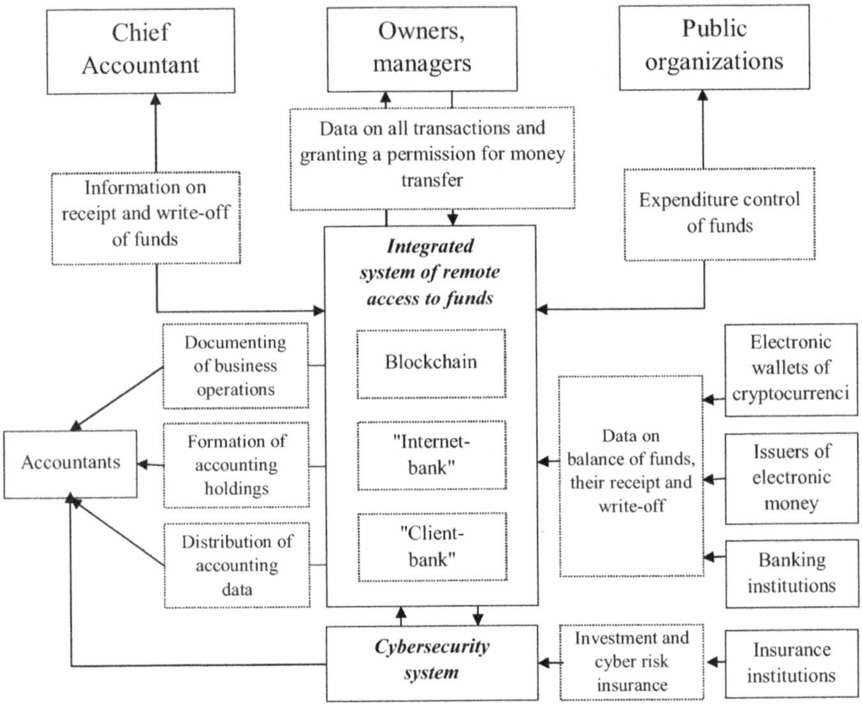

Fig. 2.4. System of accounting and cybersecurity of non-cash transfers using cryptocurrencies and other electronic money

Source: developed by the author.

The phenomenon of cryptocurrency and other electronic money forms a significant potential for automation of accounting at an enterprise. The cryptocurrency gradually acquires practical application and becomes an effective means of money turnover, which requires its recognition from the perspective of the theory of economics and accounting as an equivalent of monetary funds.

The need to use cash as a means of payment and the cash register as an organizational unit in the organizational structure of the enterprise is reduced with the use of a hybrid system. Cash can be obtained at ATMs. The number of employees who operate with cash and have access to accounting information is significantly reduced, which has a positive impact on the company's cybersecurity. All information processes are performed without the direct participation of accounting professionals, which minimizes the impact of the human factor on the cybersecurity of the enterprise.

In a hybrid system, it is advisable to store e-wallet data to gain access to the balance of cryptocurrencies. According to statistics, about 25% of cryptocurrency owners have lost access keys (Value of cryptocurrency theft worldwide from 2016 to 2020). The use of a hybrid system prevents the loss of access keys to the e-wallet and, accordingly - all cryptocurrencies.

Similarly, it is advisable to provide a function of monitoring random transactions by users. It is necessary to set a time lag between debiting funds from the sender's account and crediting the recipient. During this period of time, accounting or management staff can check the correctness of payment details and, in case of error, cancel the final execution of the electronic transaction.

In the hybrid system, it is also advisable to provide insurance of investment and cyber risks. When transferring electronic funds to a cryptocurrency exchange, their owner does not actually own the assets, but gains access to them when entering the information system. In the event of a cyber attack on the information system of the exchange, the loss of cybercurrency is possible. If the exchange declares itself bankrupt, the return of cyber assets is no possible. Similarly, significant reduction in the value of cybercurrency can lead to significant losses for their owners. It is useful and effective to insure various types of risks in the process of storage and operation of cryptocurrencies. In the hybrid system, it is advisable to place proposals from various insurance companies for insurance of cryptocurrencies. The owner of cryptocurrency on a competitive basis can choose the optimal insurance set.

2.3. Use of Internet of Things technology in accounting automation and cybersecurity

Digitization of socio-economic processes is based on the widespread use of the Internet network. Stakeholder's access to the global communications network is a guarantee of efficiency, reliability, timeliness and ergonomics of processing accounting information. Electronic communications ensure association of the information process participants in a community to share functional responsibilities. The Internet is an information integrator of information resources, databases of their storage, electronic services and information exchange technologies. The information basis of the socio-economic information cycle is the accounting system – information generator and communicator.

The growing level of household penetration of Internet technologies has led to the emergence of a new fundamental phenomenon - the Internet of Things. Internet of Things technology (IoT) is a set of knowledge about the use of software and hardware, which contains technological sensors, actuators, touch monitors and computers from elements of micro-clothing, household appliances, vehicles, production equipment, etc., which connected to the Internet to interact with the world or communicate with each other.

The implementation of IoT technology in the business processes of economic entities has caused fundamental changes primarily in the automated processing of accounting information. However, along with the positive functionality of using IoT devices, there are significant obstacles to the implementation of this technology. Providing mass open Internet access to household and industrial devices poses a threat to the enterprises functioning. Cyber threats are the result of leakage of confidential credentials, information espionage, cyber attacks, cyberterrorism, which requires the organization of an effective cyber defense system in the IoT application.

The market for IoT cybersecurity systems is growing every year and will reach $ 30.9 billion by 2025. (Fig. 2.5). The permanent annual growth of this indicator since 2016 is 15%, which indicates the prospects of research in the field of cybersecurity in the context of the IoT using.

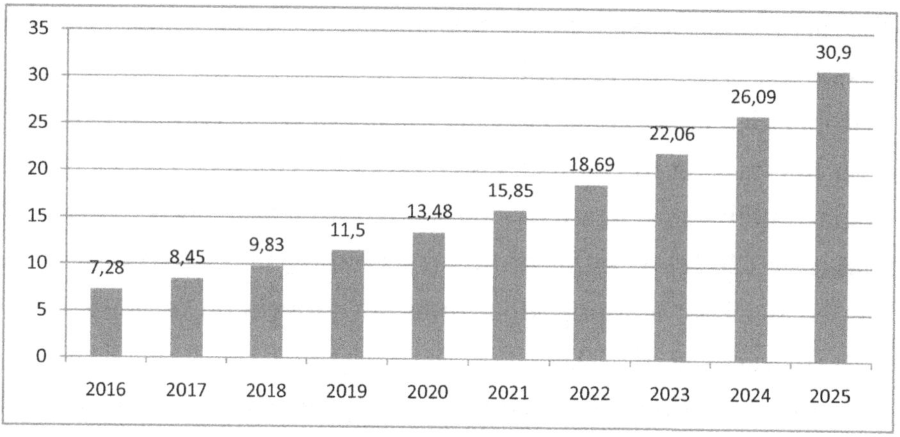

Fig. 2.5. Size of the IoT security market worldwide from 2016 to 2025 (in billion U.S. Dollars)

Source: (Size of the Internet of Things (IoT) security market worldwide from 2016 to 2025)

Numerous works devoted to cyber protection of enterprises IoT using are in the scientific space. Most of them are based on the implementation of block-chain data structuring (blockchain technology in information processing). At the same time, scientists are conducting original research on promising options for enterprises cybersecurity with IoT devices using for business purposes.

In particular, Gautam Kumar et al. substantiated the impact of Industry 4.0 on enterprises cybersecurity, which requires the use of the latest communication technologies, among which the IoT occupies an important place (Kumar et al., 2021). Nedeljko Šikanjić et al. also proposed the structure of IoT infrastructure, the use of which minimizes cyber risks and cyber threats to the operation of the enterprise (Šikanjić et al., 2021). Similarly, Matey Henry et al. explored the prospects of IoT using for cybersecurity of critical infrastructure (Henry et al., 2021). Michael Aisenberg and Esq Editor have identified state and local cybersecurity policies through a combination of IoT, cloud information processing and blockchain data structuring (Aisenberg and Editor, 2018). Similarly, Kane et al. have developed public policy areas in the field of IoT cybersecurity based on the positioning of "user values" (information needs of users) (Smith et al. 2020).

Rohani Rohan et al. explain the impact of IoT technology in consumer use on minimizing the human resource factor (Rohani, 2021). The role of artificial intelligence in cybersecurity IoT has also been explored Murat Kuzlu rt al. (2021). Continued this research by Steve Chesney et al., who proposed machine learning algorithms for prevention of active IoT cyber threats (Chesney et al., 2021).

At the same time, Amir Djenna et al. propose pragmatic strategies for cyber protection of enterprises from cyber attacks using IoT (Djenna et al., 2020). Another strategy for organizing IoT cybersecurity, which focuses on permanent changes in security settings, proposed Andres Mercado-Velazquez et al. (2021).

However, scientists reveal the theoretical and practical aspects of IoT cybersecurity from the standpoint of economic information processing. The accounting nature of most information about socio-economic processes at the enterprise is ignored in scientific research. And only a few developments simultaneously relate to accounting and cybersecurity. For example, E.E. Cohen identify the following advantages and disadvantages for the chain of business reporting of the enterprise using IoT:

– automate the information collection needed for record keeping and decision making with the potential advantage of facilitating the collection of increased amounts of information (in more detail and more often) with the reduction of manual labor errors;

– reducing the time between the event and its recording for a more timely decision;

– assistance in assessing the performance and manageability of business processes;

– increasing the amount of accounting data, the number of actions and observations, decreasing the direct human impact (Cohen, 2018).

Researcher E. Smith, who deals with modern problems of accounting computerization, identifies the following advantages of combining accounting with IoT: 1) The ability to assets monitoring; improved asset utilization; 2) Cost savings; 3) Improving quality; 4) Quantified employees - labor protection; 5) More effective income analysis; 6) Improving forecasting; 7) Improved risk management; 8) Better decision making and business efficiency (Smith, 2020).

An important ability of IoT is the data capture about events and phenomena, which is a valuable information resource for accounting and business management.

As proved by Legenchuk S.F. et al., it is necessary to consider that IoT concerns data processing from various objects which are input data from a position of accounting information systems. It's possible to state existence of influence of IoT on methods of collecting and processing of accounting data. The use of sensors to obtain primary information about things and people (accounting staff) and ensure their interconnection in the network will increase the efficiency of accounting information systems in enterprises (Lehenchuk et al., 2021).

Obtaining accounting data using IoT can occur at a significant territorial distance from the sender to the recipient of information. The place of economic activity, which is equipped with technological sensors, can be located at considerable spatial distances from the accounting and management department. Since the primary accounting data is captured and registered automatically, no need to send accounting or management staff to the place of occurrence of the economic activity facts.

The use of IoT minimizes the involvement of accounting professionals in the process of collecting primary data. Identification, capturing, registration and primary processing of information take place with the use of technological sensors that are part of the IoT. Since most information processes are fully automated, the need to involve human resources in the organization of accounting is reduced. Uncertainty, likelihood of errors, financial fraud, inaccuracies, non-compliance with deadlines, etc. are related to the human factor. As a result, accounting data are captured using Internet-connected equipment with a high level of cybersecurity. Reducing the impact of the human factor on information processes is the key to effective organization of control over the functioning of enterprises.

The IoT using transforms the process of providing audit services. Audit companies gain confidence in the accuracy of accounting data obtained using modern computer and communication technologies. Auditors may skip the stage of documentary verification of the financial and economic activities of the enterprise, as most of the accounting data is collected in electronic form. Similarly, conducting inventory and other types of material inspections is greatly simplified with the use of technological sensors. Information about the actual availability of assets or liabilities of the company is automatically compared with the accounts on a permanent basis. The informing of accounting and auditing workers with formation of inventory descriptions is carried out at the moment of detection of deviations. Most audit procedures can be performed remotely from the auditee. Distancing in the implementation of audit services is useful in the pandemic expectations of society.

Accounting and auditing professionals also receive real-time accounting information through the IoT using. Global electronic communications significantly minimizes the time lag between the occurrence of accounting information and their transmission to the accounting department. As a result, automatically captured accounting information is always timely and up-to-date. There are significant cyber threats to the operation of the enterprise due to the need for permanent connection of technological sensors to the Internet (Table 2.2).

Table 2.2

Internet of things (IoT) security threats and concerns worldwide

№	**Internet of things (IoT) security threats and concerns**	%
1.	Attacks on IoT devices that may impact critical operations	33
2.	Lack of skilled personnel to implement IoT security	32
3.	Protecting sensitive data generated by an IoT device (encryption, tokenization, etc.)	31
4.	Identifying or discovering sensitive data generated by an IoT device	27
5.	Loss or theft of IoT devices	27
6.	Lack of security frameworks and controls within the IoT environment	26
7.	Privacy violations related to data generated by an IoT device	26
8.	Lack of effective access controls/device authentication	26
9.	Lack of industry standards for securing IoT devices	25
10.	Validating the integrity of data collected by IoT devices (device identity, provisioning)	7
11.	Privileged user access to IoT devices	2

Source: (Internet of things (IoT) security threats and concerns worldwide)

First of all, cyberattacks focus on restricting or stopping access to the Internet to cause critical damage to businesses (33% of the global number of cyberattacks). Loss of Internet access can not only block the transfer of collected accounting data, but also lead to the complete suspension of business entities. The management of the entity should provide backup sources of connection to the global communications network. Duplex Internet access through cable providers and cellular operators is helpful to prevent unexpected Internet access.

There is a possibility of credentials being stolen and then passed to third parties, because IoT sensors and devices are connected to the Internet. IoT devices can be used by attackers for personal and industrial espionage. For example, items of clothing with Internet connection functions are able to collect information about the location, biological parameters of life and personal electronic communications of enterprise personnel.

However, the same data can be useful for managing the activities of accounting professionals in the process of performing their functional duties. It is advisable to monitor the time of staff performance of certain functional work or procedures. Based on the operogram of the working day of specialists, it is possible to determine ways to optimize the employees functioning. It's possible to determine the amount of wages of full-time and employees of the enterprise using information from personal IoT-devices about the time worked. The cost of services of third-party (outsourcing) accounting or auditing institutions also depends on the number of working man-hours.

Information about the employee's work with IoT-devices, which came to third parties, can be used to clarify the mechanism of pricing of professional services by accounting and auditing firms, which is part of non-competitive. Instead, IoT technology sensors built into production equipment can also send accounting data to attackers. The reason for the cyber threats high level for interception of accounting data by third parties is the not enough attention to the use of safety passwords for access to IoT devices. The management of the enterprise omits in the security policy the moments of change of standard logins and passwords when using technological sensors and devices. It is recommended to develop specific regulations for the use of cryptographic security systems, frequent changes in the identification methods for access to IoT devices. Emphasis on cybersecurity should be carried out in two ways: personal protection of individual IoT devices of enterprise employees and global protection of accounting information obtained from technological sensors of production equipment.

Intruders can change the parameters of their work after accessing IoT technology devices. Third parties receive full control of economic processes serviced by technological equipment. There may be disruptions in the implementation of business cycles, deliberate deterioration of product quality, excessive consumption of production resources, decommissioning of equipment, which will lead to increased costs of the enterprise and economic bankruptcy.

More threatening to enterprises cybersecurity is to increase access rights for current employees of the enterprise or granting these rights to third parties for the purpose of unauthorized entry into the enterprise territory. IoT-damaged devices, which are a technological part of the enterprise's security system, can authenticate third parties with the right to access confidential information. Third parties are potentially capable of espionage, sabotage, terrorism and destructive acts when entering the company's divisions.

Preventive avoidance of adverse events for cybersecurity requires multi-stage identification of persons requesting the right to intervene in the information or territorial space of the enterprise. It is advisable to carry out automatic authentication of persons in parallel with the use of IoT devices and confirmation by employees of the security department of the right to access particularly important and confidential information of the enterprise. It is recommended to control by security officers of the correctness of the automatic access system at the points of physical crossing of the enterprises territory. Additional involvement of human resources in the cyber defense of the enterprise minimizes the risks of third-party impact on IoT devices, on the use of which the technological component of the cybersecurity of the enterprise is based..

Monitoring of communication channels and routes is also important to ensure the cyber protection of accounting data. It is advisable to control the compliance of information flows to the pre-established scheme of accounting information. Confidential information is suspected if discrepancies are found. The transfer of information from the capturing place to the database should take place through regulated communication channels. The use of unreliable electronic communications calls into question the accuracy of accounting information, which may cause the loss of its consumer value.

The permanent inflow of Big data from IoT-devices creates a significant information load on the software and hardware resources of the enterprise. Processing of significant information arrays requires the introduction of the latest computer-communication form of accounting in the activities of enterprises. This form of accounting can be adapted to the growing network of electronic communications of the enterprise, which eliminates such communication barriers as: duplication, inconsistency of different information sources, competition, poor perception, ambiguity, improper comparability of accounting information, etc.

Attackers can also use IoT devices for DoS / DDoS attacks, which lead to the failure of the normal operation of software and hardware. IoT devices can generate random requests to an automated accounting system, which can block the processing of accounting information. Ensuring cybersecurity of the enterprise requires the use of methods to prevent and eliminate the effects of DoS / DDoS cyber attacks not only on the computer equipment of the enterprise, but also on all devices that are part of IoT technology. An additional way to organize the cyber protection of accounting resources is their separation from other types of information that have no customs value for the management of the enterprise. For example, technical information from technological sensors of production equipment should be sent separately to the organizational and technical departments of the enterprise and so on.

The main directions of using IoT technology to overcome cyber threats in the accounting and cybersecurity are shown in Fig. 2.6.

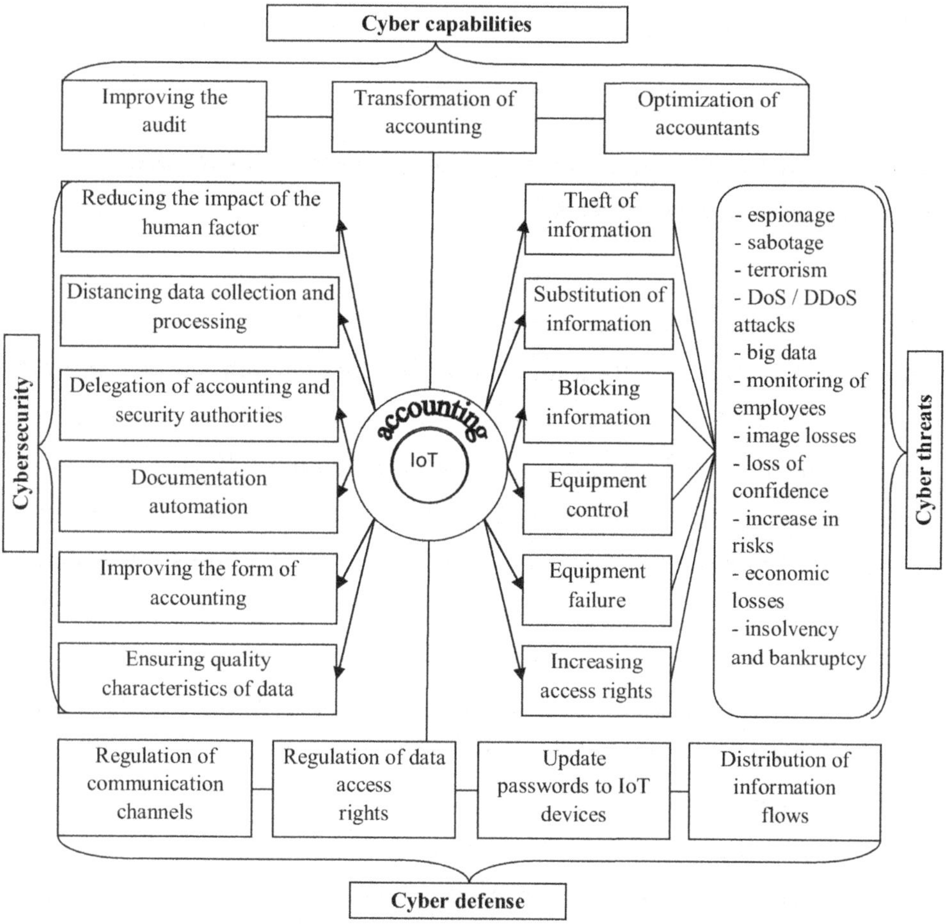

Fig. 2.6. The use of Internet of Things technology for accounting and cybersecurity

Source: developed by the author.

The use of IoT technology in accounting creates opportunities to avoidance threats to the enterprises functioning for cybersecurity ensuring. Realizing the benefits of using IoT devices creates favorable conditions for enterprises cybersecurity. Instead, the risks of implementing IoT technology are significantly minimized provided the effective organization of accounting in the enterprise as a basis for establishing cybersecurity of information flows.

2.4. Accounting of wages with the use of biometrics to ensure cybersecurity of enterprises

Business entities often use a checkpoint system to allow employees to enter the premises. Establishing a checkpoint mechanism at the enterprise provides control over the presence of personnel at the workplace and prevention of fraud or theft of material values. In the conditions of digitalization of accounting and management of economic activity, the automated checkpoint system is used for granting admission to personnel, allowing entry to vehicles or permitting movement of materials through checkpoints to zones with restricted access (Avtomatyzovana systema kontroliu dostupu). The technical elements of the automated checkpoint system include regular and wall mount turnstiles; turnstiles for passage in corridors; man-trap cubicles; automatic doors; rotary turnstiles; revolving doors; road blockers; barriers; parking systems; round sliding doors; full height turnstiles; sliding turnstiles, video surveillance cameras, etc. (Avtomatyzovana systema kontroliu dostupu), which are installed at the intersection of the enterprise or functional premises. The system operates on the principle of personalized identification of personnel at the time of crossing the information-spatial boundaries of the enterprise. A unique identifier in most cases is an individual chip card with personal data of the employee.

The automated system registers the arrival and departure of the worker and thus calculates his actual working time. In practice, as noted by A.V. Yanchev, various methods of automated collection and processing of information on labour and wages accounting are used. Their choice largely depends, on the one hand, on the type of production, the peculiarities of its organization and technology; organization and forms of remuneration; applied forms of primary documents and their templates; systems of centralized, decentralized or mixed accounting, forms of accounting; on the other hand, on the type, class, hardware of the used computers and accessories; methods of organizing information support; degree of digitalization and automation of normative-planned calculations, etc. (Yanchev, 2015).

However, the effectiveness of such accounting remains questionable in the case if an employee is present on the company premises, but is not performing their functional duties. The employee may be in a location that does not directly fall within the scope of his competence. In other words, the presence of a person at work does not guarantee the performance of his professional duties, which cannot be considered an effective way of accounting for time worked and wages. Additionally, individual card of an employee may be used by another person, thus violating the principle of personal employee authentication. To avoid organizational and functional limitations of automated personnel authentication for the purposes of accounting of working time and wages, it is advisable to use modern biometrics technology. Biometrics is a set of automated methods and means of human identification based on their physiological or behavioural characteristics (Biometriia).

Biometric authentication technology is gaining considerable popularity in commercial use. According to a study that Global Biometrics in Workforce Management Market conducted in 2019 among companies in North America and Europe that use modern computer and communication technologies, 62% of respondents use biometric authentication capabilities (with 86% projected in 2021). Most businesses (51%) use biometrics through smart phones. However, systems of time clocks (20%), smart locks to premises (18% - access to server equipment and 14% - access to office premises), portable devices as items of clothing (5%) and others are increasingly used (Fig. 2.7) (Global Biometrics in Workforce Management Market, 2019).

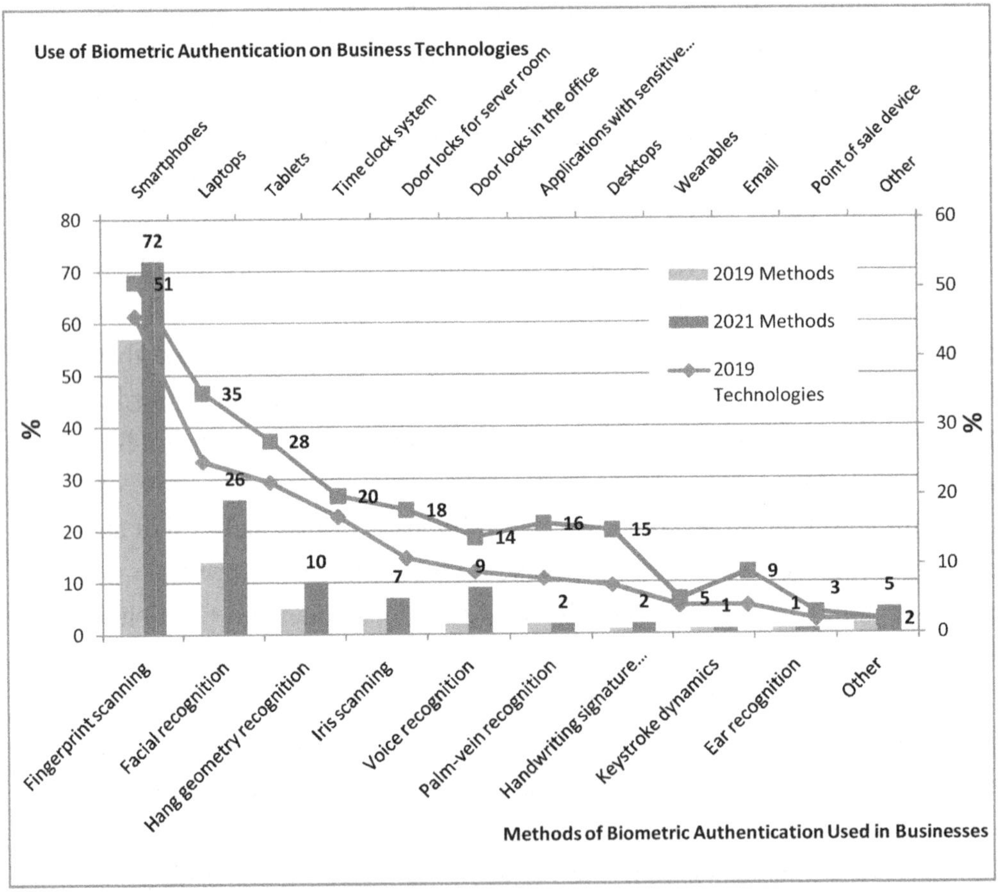

Fig. 2.7. Technologies and methods of biometric authentication in business Source: (Global Biometrics in Workforce Management Market, 2019).

Other business entities, when planning the introduction of biometric authentication technologies for employees, take into account organizational and functional barriers and risks (Table 2.3). According to the IT experts surveyed by Global Biometrics in Workforce Management Market, the most significant barriers are significant cost of technology (67%) and reliability (59%), while the biggest risks are the possibility of false positives (64%) and fraud with replication of identifier (57%). These limitations in the implementation of biometrics are solved with further scientific and technical development of the technology. However, overcoming the next barrier (the need for biometric data management - 47%) and risk (lack of standards and methods of data use - 50%) requires research in the field of practical use of biometric authentication technologies, in particular for business purposes.

Table 2.3

Barriers and Concerns (Lacks) to Adopting Biometric Authentication in the Workplace

Biggest Barriers to Adopting Biometric Authentication in the Workplace	**% interviewers**	**Security Concerns About Using Biometric Authentication in the Workplace**	**% interviewers**
Cost of technology	67	Risks of false positives	64
Reliability concerns	59	Identifiers can be replicated	57
Management of biometric data	47	Lack of standards and using methods	50
System upgrade requirements	42	Risks of stolen biometric data	48
Employee push back	42	Compliance risks	37
Complexity of transition	40	Identifiers cannot be revoked	35
End user training requirements	38	Other	6

Source: (Global Biometrics in Workforce Management Market, 2019).

Studying the possibilities of economic use of biometric authentication technology, scientists have determined that developments in the field of collecting data on working hours and location of the company's staff are particularly promising. For example, I. Fubara-Manuel investigated the method of using biometric authentication technologies to control the movement of personnel of enterprises, the entrance (exit) beyond the perimeter of various premises or areas (Fubara-Manuel, 2020). B. Li, G. Ponson, Y. Ezzahi investigated the security aspects of identifying the spatial movements of personnel and its impact on access to information and material resources, which determine the relevance of biometrics in ensuring cybersecurity of the enterprise (Ponson and Ezzahi, 2020). In continuation of cybersecurity research, S. Sinno and C. Hawley scientifically explained the means of controlling access to information based on biometric authentication in terms of monitoring the work of employees (Sinno and Hawley, 2020). Similarly, Sun Zhenjun et al. highlight the potential of using personal authentication for more than merely monitoring movement within the premises – for determining the actual time of functional duties' performance (Sun Zhenjun et al., 2021). This research was continued by S. Boonkrong, who identified the features of remuneration based on the monitoring of employees' access to computer equipment through logins and passwords (Boonkrong, 2021).

Biometric authentication is actively used in software and hardware of working time control systems and to ensure compliance with labour discipline. The main functions of such systems include:

- establishing work schedules of the enterprise (organization) as a whole, its structural subdivisions and employees;
- calculating the amount of time worked by employees according to their work schedules;
- identifying deviations from work schedules (abnormal situations);
- controlling access of employees to the enterprise premises, etc. (Systema obliku robochoho chasu «STOP-Time 4.0», 2016).

However, both working time control systems and scientific works of researchers on personal biometric authentication do not consider the possibility of automating the accounting and control of working hours and salaries of employees of business entities. At the same time, scholars ascertain new trends in the automation of accounting for employee payments caused by the development of communication technologies and remote mode of work precipitated by the pandemic. In particular, L. Ocheretko and H. Udovychenko consider the transformation of the work process and the peculiarities of wage accounting in a time of global pandemic (Ocheretko and Udovychenko, 2020). G. Neil identified the main trends in non-monetary wages, which involves the transition to teleworking and remuneration in electronic currencies, along with the automation of payroll (Neil, 2012). The main trend in the workflow is the implementation of information and communication technologies to ensure remote or isolated performance of functional responsibilities. J. Fletcher et al. also emphasize the need to restrict access to the company's premises to ensure employee biosecurity, which requires changes in accounting and workflow management (Fletcher et al., 2020).

W. Gupta has developed a unique model for determining the amount of potential salary based on the assessment of professional and personal characteristics of applicants on the list of vacancies on employment sites (Gupta, 2020). Similarly, based on the technology of "deep learning", Jong-Yih Kuo et al proposed a method of automated determination and accounting of wages based on a number of variables for arbitrary periods of time (Kuo, 2021).

According to V. I. Revenok and O. S. Mamchur, something all scientists share is the attempt to outline the requirements for an accounting system of wages and working time that uses computer communication technologies:

- integration of personnel accounting, labour accounting and its payment into a single whole;

- centralization of processing of information on labour accounting and its payment;

- automated collection of information about employees' work and time worked by them;

- automation of typical payment transactions;

- automated control over the movement of employees on the enterprise premises and access to information (Revenok and Mamchur, 2015).

Biometric scanners are the technical component of the automated checkpoint system; they are installed at the intersection of the designated areas of the enterprise, production and office premises. Production equipment and computerized workplaces are also equipped with biometric authentication of employees. Each unit of fixed assets is assigned a list of responsible persons who are given access to information and performance of official duties. An automated employee authentication system in most cases is used for security reasons.

It is proposed to also use the information on the authorized access to the enterprise premises and equipment in order to record the time worked by staff. Biometric authentication of employees in the process of using machines and tools is regarded as the performance of official duties. Time spent operating equipment can be recognized as working time of the employee, which affects the calculation of wages. A similar principle of estimating time worked is already applied in automated workstations of computer specialists, whose working day (clocking in and out) is determined through personal identification.

The main problem in the automation of time tracking is the control over the work of employees who may be at their workstations, but are not performing functional duties. The use of video surveillance is quite effective in this case. Visual identification provides control over the movement of workers between locations and time spent at the enterprise to ensure its cybersecurity.

In addition, an automated checkpoint system based on biometric authentication of personnel is useful for demarcating human flows within the premises of the enterprise in order to provide biological protection. Controlling overcrowding and personal hygiene indoors is an important component of preventing and avoiding biological threats in a COVID-19 pandemic.

The list of constant and variable data on the movement of personnel within the premises and buildings of an enterprise obtained using biometrics technology for the purposes of accounting and cybersecurity is given in the information model in Fig. 2.8.

It is advisable to use a single database as the basis of an automated system of time worked accounting. The integrated database should contain all information about the company's employees: age, experience, qualifications, education, job title, job responsibilities, authorization to access information, methods of calculating wages, available wage tax benefits, special conditions that determine the right to bonuses or compensations. All documents related to personnel policy are entered into the information system.

To ensure the reliability and timeliness of accounting and control procedures in enterprises that use biometric authentication systems, it is recommended to choose the minute as the basic unit of measurement of time worked. Minute of working time is the optimal unit of calculation that allows for a more efficient accounting of wages. In addition, the use of minute-by-minute accounting enables detailed control over worker delays, absences from workstations or unauthorized access to restricted areas of the enterprise during working hours. At the end of the reporting period, based on data on total unproductive loss of working time, it is recommended to automatically deduct wages.

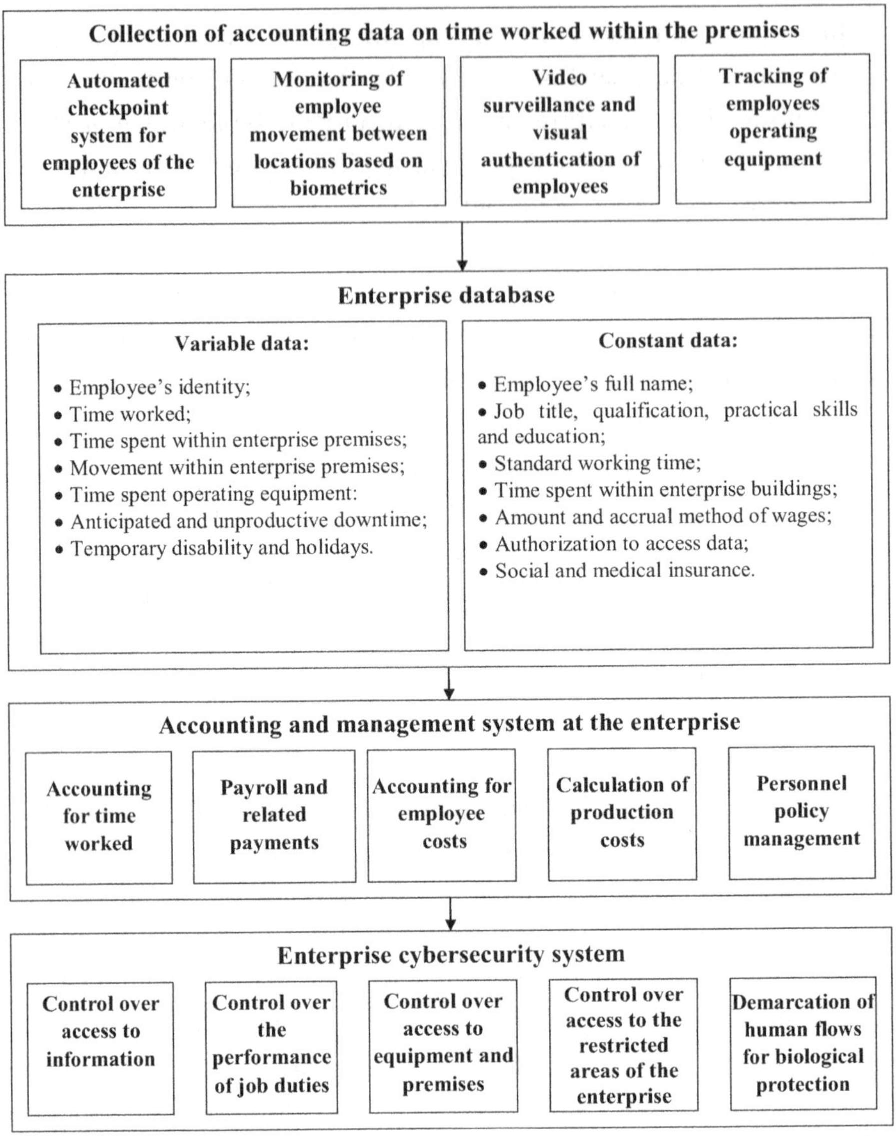

Fig. 2.8. Information model of automated accounting of time worked and wages based on biometric authentication systems to ensure cybersecurity

Source: developed by the author.

Information on the personal deviation of the working time from the normative indicators should be promptly sent to staff. Every employee has the opportunity to self-correct and adjust working hours. The possibility of an employee manipulating the accounting information is minimized by eliminating independent filling of time-sheets and thus rounding up to full working hours. The biometric authentication system can automatically record the start and end time of an employee's working time, which ensures a fair determination of wages and minimizes conflicts between employees and employers.

Accounting of working time in minutes can be used to stimulate productivity of employees with a regulatory working time. Per-minute accounting of time worked is relevant for employees whose wages depend on a combined performance of different types of work within the planned time period. In particular, there is a possibility of reliable accounting and control of working hours for employees with irregular hours working from home with hourly wages during the COVID-19 pandemic. The employee independently monitors and determines the duration of the work shift.

Additionally, biometric authentication of employees makes it possible to record the time worked accurately even if there are gaps between shifts, which is relevant for companies with three-shift operation. Employees can leave the premises of the enterprise (including to perform tasks from home) or step out of the production buildings for a certain time. The system will identify the fact of relocation and calculate the total time of performing direct functional duties. It is necessary to keep separate records of employee downtime that is caused by the technological process or the specifics of the enterprise. In the time regulations of the automated accounting system it is necessary to prescribe that there may be stretches in the production process when the employee is not perming their functional duties, which do not constitute loss of working time. For example, after the production of a certain volume of products, it takes time to cool the equipment, load a new portion of raw materials and so on. In other words, after the end of the production cycle, the employee in accordance with job descriptions can leave the workstation or production premises and use the forced downtime for their own needs.

Automated control is provided over personal unproductive losses of time, tracking of deviations from the normative indicator of time necessary for performance of one production task, production of one unit of finished goods by the employee, rendering of services, etc. Each fact of deviation should be recorded in a single database in different analytical sections. Accumulated data are the basis for identifying the instances of reduced productivity of each employee, which may be a signal to review their working conditions or prompt retraining.

It is possible to automatically calculate the salaries of staff based on the information about the time spent within the enterprise premises or at home. To automate the accounting and control of wages, it is advisable to pre-fix the tariff for the unit of time worked for each type of production facility, as well as remote performance of functional duties. Thus, it is necessary to set the basic tariff rates for employees for each minute of stay in a certain type of premises (at home), for which it is recommended to divide the enterprise premises into several areas. In addition, it is necessary to restrict the access of personnel to certain types of buildings or territory of the enterprise to ensure cyber and biological security.

Wages should be calculated taking into account the functional purpose of the premises and the professional responsibilities of the employee. Quite often, the area of the enterprise, which is the main workstation of one employee, can be ancillary to another. Therefore, the enterprise territory should be divided into separate functional areas for each group of staff. It is also necessary to develop a timetable for each employee of the enterprise by determining the impact on the payroll of time worked, productive and unproductive downtime. As a result, the employees can receive detailed timed instructions for performing functional duties, moving around the company and working from home. Regulating time parameters of work helps to avoid excessive concentration of workers on the enterprise premises, thus minimizing biological threats (especially the risk of contracting COVID-19).

It is also useful to automatically compare time standards and indicators of actual time worked. In case of overtime work, it is advisable to automatically accrue additional pay to employees. If the length of a working day is fixed, it is advisable to offer compensation for overtime work. Similarly, the enterprise management can use extra pay in addition to wages to stimulate remote performance of functional duties from home. In this case, both biological risks and employee costs are reduced.

The use of a minute as a calculation unit should start with the second hour of overtime. Since in the first minutes after the end of the working day employees may spend time on interpersonal communication or personal hygiene, it is impractical to classify the delay in leaving the workplace as overtime. Therefore, incentive payments should be made for the full first hour and subsequent minutes of overtime.

The work of employees at night and on weekends is also subject to monitoring. It is advisable to automatically calculate the basic and additional wages by comparing the actual time of employees spend in the workplace (remotely performing their functional duties from home), at their workstation or operating equipment.

Similarly, it is possible to control the performance of functional responsibilities from home through permanent monitoring of all operations occurring from remote workstations. The time the employee spends working in specialized software or performing tasks on the Internet (provided for by their job description) is subject to control. Time of long downtimes, consuming entertainment, using social media, etc. is excluded from the total employee working time and wages.

Primary documents like timesheets and payroll can be filled out electronically using the accounting data from the system of biometric employee authentication. It is recommended to send payment slips automatically to the employee workstations or personal emails in order to inform them about the method of calculating wages and deductions from it.

The very fact of forming payroll registers can start the automatic process of making payments to employees. It is advisable to form the appropriate bank documents with a pre-set time lag after registration of information on accrued wages in the system. After receiving electronic approvals from the officials responsible for such transactions, payment documents are automatically sent to the executor through the banking communications system. The bank transfers funds to personal salary accounts of employees, which completes the cycle of accrual and payment of wages.

In addition to the company's staff, information about the working time and wages from the biometric employee authentication system should be automatically sent to interested stakeholders. Accounting information in addition to internal purposes can be used for: verification of sick leaves when calculating compensation under the terms of social and medical insurance; formation of generalized statistical arrays of data on the number of employees and wages; confirmation of the accuracy of taxes and contributions to social insurance funds, etc.

It is also recommended to use the biometric authentication system to account for the company's employee costs. Prior to the beginning of the COVID-19 pandemic, the costs of social, residential and recreational support for employees were increasing. Innovative enterprises actively created common use areas, which, in addition to corridors, toilets, and bathrooms also included playrooms, lecture halls, meeting rooms, etc. The structure of employee costs has changed with the increase in remote and isolated performance of functional responsibilities. It is also incorrect to account for the cost of maintaining premises for employees who perform functional duties remotely. Given the free access of all employees to common areas, as well as the transfer of workstation of some employees outside the company, it is difficult to effectively distinguish the employee costs from production, administrative, marketing or other costs.

If the total number of specialists who were physically present in the common use areas is identified, the employee costs can automatically be distributed between different groups of specialists. In other words, the total cost of operating the premises at the end of the reporting period can be grouped in proportion to the number of visitors from production, administrative, sales and other groups of personnel during the reporting period. The employee costs for those working outside the company premises are not taken into account.

Information from the biometric authentication system on the number and positions of employees who visited the dining area is the basis for automated accounting of employee costs. The cost of food in canteens, bars, cafes that is fully or partially funded by the company should be automatically attributed to several groups by specialization. After the end of the work shift or calendar day, it is recommended to categorize the total cost of food into different types in proportion to the number of visitors and their positions. Using biometrics technology provides reliable cost accounting without the need for fictitious distribution among all employees (including those at home) or attribution to only one group (item) of costs.

Information from the biometric authentication system on the time worked by production workers and their wages can also be used as an optimal basis for the distribution of overhead costs. The need to accrue wages to employees who simultaneously work in several positions, for example in different production units for the manufacture of several types of products, is problematic for the accounting departments of enterprises. Both parallel and remote (from home) performance of functional duties negatively affects the reliability of the distribution of overhead costs in proportion to the wages of production staff. On the other hand, biometric authentication of employees that records their performance of exclusively production duties contributes to the optimization of accounting and distribution of overhead costs in the enterprise. Similarly, automation can be introduced for all costs associated with the sustenance and operations of employees at the enterprise after they are derived from the automated system of biometric employee authentication.

2.5. Comprehensive use of 6g cellular technology accounting activity costs and cybersecurity

Increasing of the population mobility and remote performance of official duties during the COVID-19 pandemic are creating new requirements for data transfer speed on the Internet. Modern technologies of the Internet of Things, blockchain, adaptive audio and video streaming are based on the use of high-speed wireless electronic communications. Support of wireless cellular communication is implemented in modern wearable, household and industrial technological devices. Data collection and management of functional processes takes place remotely in a permanent mode via the Internet. Modern technologies of 4G cellular networks are not able to meet the needs of users in large data sets with a minimum time lag, which hinders the digitalization of social and economic processes.

Theoretical research and applied developments on the use of the fifth generation cellular networks are being actively conducted. 5G cellular technology enables full broadcasting of social and economic calculations in the cloud environment, use of blockchain technology on all technical devices, integration of technological equipment into a single production information network, etc. Instead, the economic use of developments in the field of artificial intelligence, total virtualization of communications, unmanned aerial vehicles and autopilot of vehicles, connection to the

Internet of all technical devices determines the achievable horizon of the new sixth generation of cellular communication (Fig. 2.9).

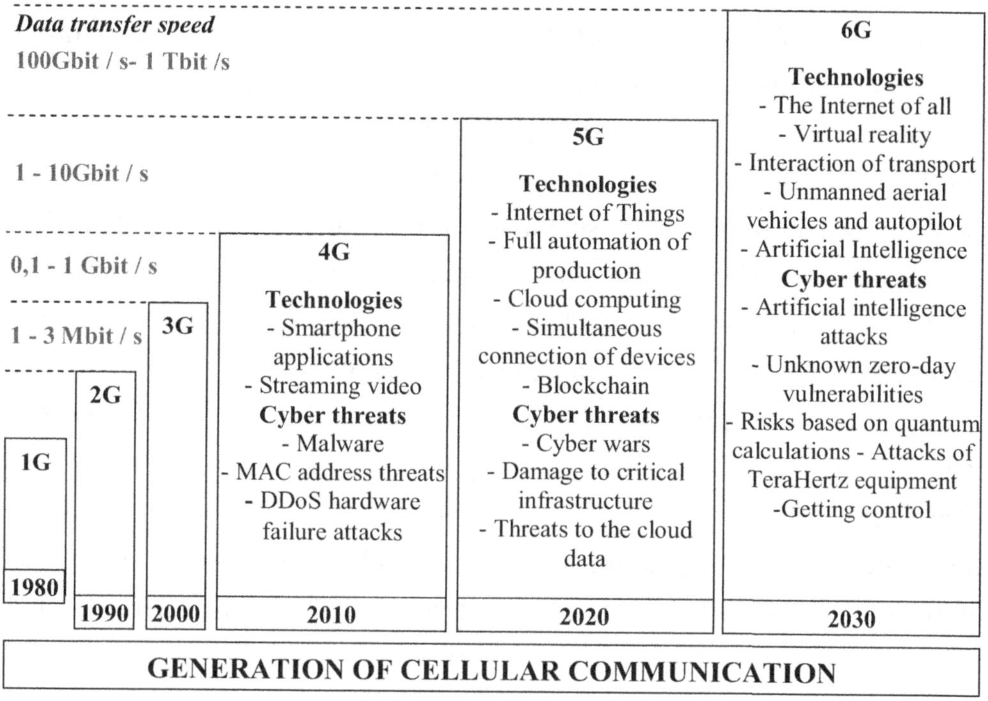

Fig. 2.9. Development of cellular networks of mobile communications

Source: generated by the author based on (Mobile broadband subscriptions worldwide 2007-2020)

With the development of cellular generations, cyber threats, which are actual for the economic activity of most businesses, are becoming more complicated. In previous generations of cellular networks, telecommunication companies are responsible for cybersecurity. Cellular network operators are investing heavily in software and hardware for cybersecurity systems, increasing the number of security personnel, and investigating cyber incidents. In the conditions of implementation of 6G technology at the micro level, the functions of cybersecurity are partially transferred to the management of economic entities. In management the need for ensuring cybersecurity of telecommunications equipment installed in the premises (on the territory) of an enterprise arise. The direct exchange of information within the 6G cellular communication is the full responsibility of employees of an enterprise, and therefore it requires additional measures for implementing effective cybersecurity.

The range of problemsof providing effective cybersecurity in conditions of the use of 6G cellular communications is the subject of scientific research of many scientists. Lu, Yang studied the historical development of cyber threats from cellular communications from 1G to 5G, which allowed to identify the trends in cybersecurity in terms of 6G technology (Yang, 2021). The research was continued by Porambage Pawani et al., who predicted problematic aspects of the use of potential technologies in 6G cellular networks, such as: distributed ledger technology (DLT), physical layer protection, distributed artificial intelligence, THz and quantum computing, and suggested ways to ensure enterprise cybersecurity (Porambage et al., 2021). Russell Huang, and Grant Turner explored the UK's experience in providing cybersecurity from Huawei's corporation information espionage using 5G cellular technology and predicted possible 6G threats to cybersecurity (Huang and Turner, 2020). Junwei Zhang, et al. developed a scheme of decentralized information exchange using 6G cellular communication for the implementation of crowdsourcing (transfer of production and information functions to an indefinite number of people), which creates new requirements for cybersecurity (Zhang, et al., 2021).

Considerable attention is paid to improving the conceptual apparatus of scientific research in terms of providing cybersecurity in the field of 6G. Petar Popovski et al. in particular conducted in-depth research on the development of 6G cellular networks and related concepts of “simultaneousness”, “presence” and “causality”, which are the basic categories in ensuring the information security of users of telecommunications services (Popovski et al., 2021). Terminological research was also conducted by Mika Ylianttila et al. (2020) and Minghao Wang et al. (2020), who justified the positioning of the concepts of "trust", "security" and "confidentiality" in the context of creating a reliable 6G cellular connection, which involves the development of multidisciplinary technologies, regulatory techniques, technoeconomics, policy and ethics.

In the scientific space, there are diverse studies of the subject use of 6G cellular technologies in combination with cybersecurity of business entities. For example, Yushan Siriwardhana et al. substantiated the significant level of penetration of artificial intelligence mechanisms into the operation of 6G, which creates significant cyber risks in the activities of operators and users of cellular communications. At the same time, scientists point out that artificial intelligence is able to avoid and prevent the manifestation of cyber threats in the functioning of economic entities (Siriwardhana et al., 2021). The integration of blockchain and 6G technologies, in the opinion of Ali Hussain Khan et al., creates opportunities for effective information protection through decentralization of cellular networks and distributed access to databases. Researchers have explored different ways of combining blockchain technology with the use of 6G cellular communications, which helps to optimize cybersecurity (Khan et al., 2021).Miloslav Hoschek explained the impact of quantum cybersecurity on the operation of critical infrastructure based on the use of 5G and, in the long run, 6G (Hoschek, 2021). Similar studies were conducted by H. Al-Mohammed and E. Yaacoub on the prospects for the development of Internet of Things technology in the era of 6G cellular communications, which requires the use of quantum computing and communications (Al-Mohammed and Yaacoub, 2021).

The generalization of the authors' scientific achievements makes it possible to identify cyber risks that threaten 6G cellular networks: attacks with the use of artificial intelligence, previously unknown "Zero Day", risks based on quantum calculations, attacks with the use of fast (Tera

Hertz) equipment etc., physical attacks to wiretap on telephony, etc., which requires improvements in cybersecurity methods and micro-levels.

The presence of significant cyber risks of using the technology of cellular communication of new generations is an obstacle to their widespread use, which can be seenin Fig. 2.10.

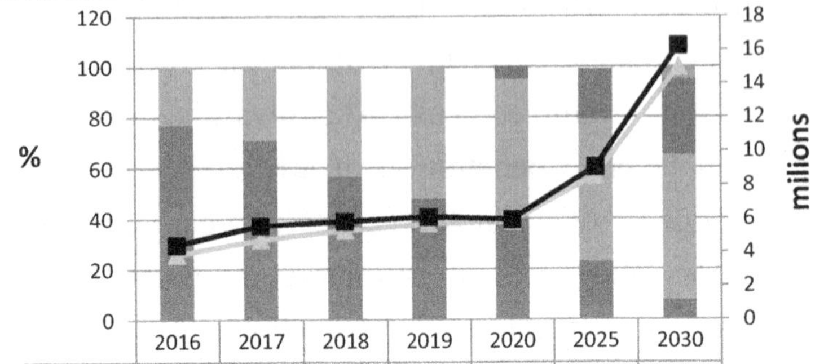

	2016	2017	2018	2019	2020	2025	2030
6G	0	0	0	0	0	0	5
5G	0	0	0	0	5	20	30
4G	23	29	43	52	55	56	57
3G	32	31	28	25	20	18	8
2G	45	40	29	23	20	5	0
Year-over-year growth	0,581	0,861	0,563	0,415	0,124	0,537	1,290
Mobile broadband subscriptions	3,863	4,724	5,287	5,702	5,826	8,513	14,965

Fig. 2.10. The rate of distribution of cellular devices by generation (2G-6G)

Source: determined on the basis of (Mobile technology share by generation 2016-2025); the figure for 2030 is calculated based on data forecasting using Excel spreadsheets

The number of devices connected to cellular communication is increasing every year (from 3.863 million in 2016 to 5.826 million in 2020). The permanent growth of the popularity of cellular devices is partly explained by the development of new generations of cellular 4G communications (share in 2020 comprised 55%) and 5G (share in 2020 comprised 5%). However, it is necessary to take into account the insufficient future pace of introduction of the fifth and sixth generation cellular communications. In particular, if the share of 4G popularity has increased by 32% during 5 years, then the projected growth in the use of 5G technology in 2020-2025 is only 15% against the background of the popularization of the Internet of Things technology connected to the cellular Internet. Similar figures are expected and for the use of 6G technology. Improper tempos of implementation of 5G and 6G technology is explained by the lack of thorough complex research on the applied application of the cellular networks of new generation in combination with cybersecurity of economic (including accounting) information, which is also an obstacle to the widespread use of innovative technologies.

The key characteristics of 5G and 6G technologies is the reliable location of the cellular subscriber. Similarly, global satellite positioning (GPS) technology can identify the spatial location of a smartphone and, consequently, its owner. If GPS navigation provides two-dimensional information about the location and movement of the controlled object, then cellular networks promote three-dimensional positioning. In other words, based on 5G and 6G technologies, it is possible to determine the height of the cell phone in the open space or on top of the building – indoors.

Another important possibility of next-generation cellular networks is the direct exchange of information between technical devices. Without the involvement of base stations, smartphones are able to exchange data with other devices that have access to cellular communications. Direct communications provide operational and complete data, which is a valuable information resource for accounting and management purposes. Functional abilities of using 6G technology in terms of automation of processing and cyber protection of accounting information are shown in Fig. 2.11.

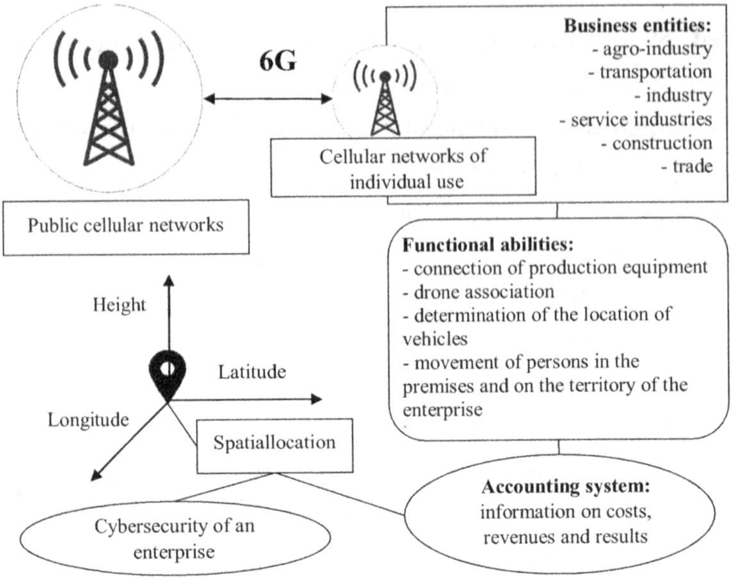

Fig. 2.11. The use of 6G cellular networks for accounting and cybersecurity of enterprises

Source: generated by the author

The use of 6G cellular communication expands the functional abilities of GPS technology in monitoring the commercial operation of vehicles. In addition to information on routes and stops of vehicles, based on 6G technology it is possible to obtain information on fuel consumption, loading (unloading), unproductive stoppage, breakages, the need for technical maintenance or repair, traffic violations, etc., which may be useful for accounting purposes and cybersecurity.

In particular, after finishing the trip, it is advisable to use the data obtained using 6G technology to account for fuels and lubricants. For each fact of moving the vehicle, it is recommended to determine the consumption of fuel (electricity) in order to reliably identify the cost of transport services. Information on the distance traveled by road in kilometers is not very informative for efficient and reliable accounting of transport costs. Different driving styles, terrain and road conditions, weight of the transported cargo significantly affect fuel consumption and, especially, electricity for electric vehicles. Therefore, only the actual fuel consumption (electricity) provided using 6G technology, and not the information on the mileage of vehicles, it is advisable to focus on the automation of accounting for transport services.

Information on timely detected facts of unproductive use of vehicles should be used for accounting and control of transport enterprises. After the identification of improper use or unplanned stoppage of vehicles during working hours, receiving fines for violations of traffic rules, it is possible to simultaneously determine those responsible for violations of employees, reflecting in the compensation for damages.

In addition to the traditional protection against vehicle theft, 6G cellular communication can be used to organize autopilot traffic. Through instant communication mechanisms based on 6G cellular networks, vehicles can avoid collisions and comply with traffic rules. In this case, it is important to ensure proper cybersecurity of vehicles for preventing unauthorized access by intruders. Using cellular networks, third parties can gain remote control of vehicles to commit further wrongdoings. Therefore, it is recommended to develop the latest protocols for cyber protection of cellular communications in combination with permanent monitoring of compliance with established routes of vehicles and traffic rules.

Together with the organization of autopilot transport of vehicles using 6G cellular communication, it is possible to provide information communication with unmanned aerial vehicles (drones). With the use ofsystems of artificial intelligence systems, it is advisable to combine drones in a swarm for collecting information for the purposes of accounting and cybersecurity of construction and agricultural enterprises. Associations (swarms) of unmanned aerial vehicles are able to monitor business activities around the clock regime without the direct participation of employees. After receiving a signal from the drone about the low battery level, a new unmanned aerial vehicle is sent for replacement. The previous drone is returned to renew the power supply, which is the basis for the permanent rotational operation of unmanned aerial vehicles.

On the basis of data on the status of construction works, it is advisable to carry out automated accounting of costs and income in accordance with the degree of completion of construction, which is justified by the construction contract. On the basis of aerovisual identification of the degree of construction works (construction of the whole building, a separate part or floor (section)) it is possible to reliably determine the cost of construction services provided. The customer of the construction of certain objects may be notified of its intermediate cost in accordance with the construction contract. Accordingly, in the accounting system it is advisable to automatically record the costs incurred, income received and the determined financial result from the provision of construction services for any period of time. Upon completion of a certain stage of construction on the basis of drone monitoring of construction works, all accounting procedures can be performed daily, which ensures the timeliness and efficiency of accounting and control.

Similarly, drones controlled via the 6G cellular network are capable of aerial visual monitoring of the process of agricultural work. The collected information on tillage, sowing process, biological transformations of plants, harvesting should be used to account for the costs of agricultural enterprises. On the basis of photos and videos it is possible to automatically determine the need for fuel and stocks, seeds, plant protection products, mineral fertilizers, etc. with automated recording in accounting. Operational accounting of material costs in an additive way ensures the formation of the intermediate cost of agricultural products.Accordingly, with the growing popularity of certain places of outdoor advertising or products (goods) may increase the cost of renting advertising and retail space. For customers of advertising signs, the cost of the service is determined individually with a clear link to the potential number of people who may be consumers of marketing activities.

Unmanned aerial vehicles are capable of automatically detecting violators of the perimeter of the territory and airspace. Based on the visual recognition of faces and comparison with the database of images of the company's staff, it is possible to identify outsiders who do not have the right to be in the security control zone. In addition to full-time employees, visual images of the faces of third parties who perform periodic work (provide services) or are visitors who receive one-time access rights are entered into the personal information database.

Unmanned aerial vehicles can also detect the presence of other third-party drones. With the massive development of small (personal) aviation, the means of air-visual espionage appear at the disposal of criminals, competitors, the media and otherpersons. In case of detection of violators of territorial and airspace, drones are notified by the security units of the enterprise to suspend illegal actions.

6G cellular communication can be implemented in any production equipment with the purpose of active transmission of production information. Regardless of the spatial location of the means of production, automated collection of production process parameters is possible. Technological data from sensors, which are equipped with fixed assets of an enterprise, it is advisable to use for automated accounting of production costs. Production equipment is able to record the quantity and quality of consumed material values and electricity (water, gas, etc.) in the process of production (works, services). All the facts of the use of objects of labor should be automatically recorded in accounting. With the use of methods of incomplete costing, it is advisable to determine quicklyall direct production costs. Calculation takes place on a permanent basis, when for each unit of finished product it is possible to determine reliablythe cost. The company's management has the opportunity to determine accurately the cost of production, which allows you to simultaneously adjust the cost of sales foreach individual order and customer.

In the operation of production equipment, it is advisable to provide a mechanism for identifying persons who are nearby. A person who visited the workplace and is not a full-time employee may be identified as a violator of the security regime. In the case of defective products, theft of raw materials, excessive consumption of resources, it is possible to identify suspects. All facts of violations are automatically reported to the security department of an enterprise.

Based on information on visits to certain types of premises, it is also recommended to determine reliablythe rent for retail space for operators. Depending on the number of people who visited the trading halls of a tenant, the amount of rent changes. At the end of the month, it is advisable to calculate and reflect in accounting the rent, which is set in proportion to the number of visitors and the area given to a tenant. Quantitative pricing option is useful for rental operators, which allows you to effectively take into account the cost of customer service not only retail space, but also areas of common use. Such premises include corridors, toilets, stairs, escalators, lounge areas, etc.

Maintenance costs of general purpose premises (heating, air conditioning, cleaning, current repairs, etc.) are mainly included in the cost of rent by retail space operators, which violates fundamental accounting principles. Instead, pricing based on the number of visitors ensures a fair distribution of such costs. In addition to commercial establishments, cost accounting based on the number of visitors should be used for catering, tourism, passenger transport services.

According to a similar method, it is possible to determine the effectiveness of outdoor advertising and the operation of shop windows in commercial establishments. Using 6G technology, the company's management receives information about popular routes of movement of visitors of trade establishments. It is recommended to determine the popularity and effectiveness of marketing activities on the basis of information about the number and duration of visitors' stops at an advertising sign or shop window. Accordingly, with the growing popularity of certain places of outdoor advertising or products (goods), the cost of renting advertising and retail spacemay increase. For customers of advertising signs, the cost of the service is determined individually with a clear link to the potential number of people who may be consumers of marketing activities.

On the other hand, it is advisable to monitor the popularity of a particular type or kind of product (goods) that are of interest to buyers, but for unknown reasons are not sold. In other words, clarification requires increasing attention to material values, which does not end with the fact of their realization. Such products (goods) require a change in pricing, sales or merchandising policy.

Quite often it is organizationally difficult to provide video surveillance and automated control of the admission of workers to the territory in the conditions of a significant flow of people or a large area of monitoring. With the use of 6G technology, it is possible to control the movement of persons through the enterprise. In the cybersecurity system of the enterprise, it is advisable to record the facts of entry of unauthorized persons using cellular communications in the premises or certain areas of the restricted area. If the violator of the information or territorial regime is promptly identified by the cybersecurity system, it is possible to prevent cybercrime.

In case of late detection of lost material or information resources, it is advisable to identify the persons involved in the offense. Based on the identification of the list of persons who were territorially near the scene of the incident for a certain period of time, it is possible to identify the offenders on the basis of identifying an individual cellular number. In the course of further investigative actions, the involvement of cellular subscribers in the cyber incident is proved. The generalized possibilities investigated and the challenges of the sixth generation cellular communication technology are given in Table 2.4.

Table 2.4

Opportunities and challenges of realized on the basis of 6G cellular technologies for cybersecurity

6G technologies	Opportunities for cyber defense	Challenges for cyber defense
Positioning	Monitoring the movement of persons through the territory, premises of an enterprise. Identification of trespassers of information regime.	The ethics of excessive control over the movement of cellular subscribers. Prevention of getting of personal data of subscribers to third parties.
Autopilot / unmannedaerial vehicles	Control over the movement and operation of commercial vehicles. Coordination of unmanned aerial vehicles in the process of aerial surveillance.	Protection against obtaining physical control over vehicles or drones by third parties.
Internet of Things	Connection of all production equipment to the Internet on the principles of Internet of Things technology for operational automatic (without employees) data collection and transmission.	Prevention of distortion and theft of information at the time of its collection and transmission.
Blockchain	Providing distributed access and data storage.	Impossibility of control by state institutions.
Quantum security	Unbreakable data encryption during transmission	Lack of the existing computing power for cellular operators. The complexity of standardization.
Artificial intelligence	Autonomous management of security system. Optimized provision of security.	Problemscalability. The difficulty of automatic identification of trespassers and informing the cybersecurity service. The need for protecting computing infrastructure at the micro level.

Source: systematized by the author

The practical implementation of the developments presented in the Table on the use of 6G cellular communication technologies (automated identification of positioning, autopilot / unmanned vehicles, Internet of Things, blockchain, quantum computing, artificial intelligence, etc.) will contribute to reliable calculation of products (works, services) and production costs of production, agricultural, construction, trade activities in combination with ensuring effective cyber protection of enterprises in terms of prevention and detection of violators of information and territorial security regime.

CHAPTER 3. ORGANIZATION OF ACCOUNTING TO ENSURE CYBER PROTECTION OF ENTERPRISES

3.1. Cybersecurity regulations of the accounting policy of the enterprise

The main regulatory document in the field of information circulation at the micro level is the accounting policy of an enterprise. It is one of the first regulations formed during the creation of any business entity, and a guide for accounting and management professionals in the implementation of accounting principles and reporting. The document on accounting policy is dominant in the regulatory and legal regulation of accounting, as it is referred to by other internal regulations.

The conditions of operating that arise from the organizational and legal form, industry, business size, etc. are indicated in the accounting policy. Important significance in the regulation of information processes has the reflection of the organizational structure of an enterprise, which directly affects the order of processing of accounting information and the formation of reporting indicators.

The accounting policy is used to providethe proof of illegal actions of the accounting and management personnel of an enterpriseby the controlling institutions. This regulatory document contains indefeasible instructions that define one of the variable methods and ways of processing accounting information. More and more companies regulate not only the methodology of financial accounting and related tax calculations, but also the peculiarities of management accounting. The accounting policy for management accounting will indicate the centers of responsibility and cost price centers, the methods for calculating and determining the cost of production, the order of formation of management reporting, etc.

Therefore, with the complication of social and economic processes, the emergence of new objects of accounting, the digitalization of the economy, the need for improving accounting policies arise. Further development of the institute of accounting regulation requires the expansion of the subject field of accounting policy. In the document on accounting policy of an enterprise it is expedient to foresee security aspects of processing of accounting information, formation and providing reports to stakeholders.

Yu.S. Tsal-Tsalko and Yu.Yu. Moroz (2017) define cybersecurity in the accounting system as the protection of the information system of an enterprise from internal and external threats, i.e. protection of an enterprise, its human and intellectual potential, information, technology, profit, added and market value of an enterprise, which is provided by a system of special actions of legal, economic, organizational, informational-technical and social character, influencing the formation of accounting policies. One of the first scientists who explained the influence of the information society and digital economy on the formation and implementation of accounting policy were M.S. Pushkar and M.T. Shchyrba (2010).

The list of components of the accounting policy in terms of its objects, subjects, goals and tasks, levels of regulation has been provided in the scientific work of I. Herasymovych (2018). The study allows to form a comprehensive understanding of the accounting policy and its significance for the operation of an enterprise in terms of transformation and digitalization of social and economic processes. Sofiia Kafka proposed to subordinate informationally various internal regulations (graphs, documents circulation, accounting automation projects and job descriptions of accounting staff) to the company's accounting policy (Kafka, 2017).

Salim Alibha et al. continued the study who substantiated the impact of accounting policies on errors in the processing of accounting information and formation of reports. In the authors' opinion, there exists a clear distinction between errors in information processing and changes in accounting principles or metods of valuatioп (Alibha et al., 2021). The need for expanding the provisions of the accounting policy (Accounting Policy 2.0) was explored by Kim Jihyun (2021), based on the transformation of US law.

Steven Harrast also proposed a list of provisions for the robotization of production processes and full automation of information processes, which should be reflected in the accounting policy of an enterprise (Harrast, 2020). Olena Lahovska and Gabriella Loskorikh (2020) explained the difference in the formation of accounting policies of IT companies from other sectors of the economy. The scientists have developed an accounting policy scheme for companies, whichoperate in the field of IT business. N. Drokina and Gulnara Kaipova determining the content of accounting policies, paid considerable attention to the provisions of automated accounting. In the opinion of the scientists, the method of automated processing of accounting information should be reflected in the document on the accounting policy of an enterprise (Drokina and Kaipova, 2020).

However, researchers focus their research on the software and hardware provisions of accounting policies for cybersecurity of an enterprise. However, the organizational aspects of cybersecurity remain beyond the attention of scientists, which determines the relevance of researches in the direction of security components of the accounting policy of an enterprise. As a result, in the accounting policy of an enterprise it is expedient to take into account security provisions for the organization of proper cyber protection of the information system of an enterprise. Security regulations are a set of requirements, rules, restrictions, procedures and responsibilities of personnel for processing and transmission of accounting information in order to achieve and maintain the state of maximum information and cybersecurity of an enterprise.

The information security of an enterprise directly depends on the effective accounting policy of an enterprise. Clear regulation in the accounting policy of accounting and management specialists for the collection, registration, processing and transmission of information significantly minimizes information threats. In the case of inadequate attention of the company's management to the communication links in the internal and external information environment, there are opportunities to manipulate registration information and steal it in order to cause damage to the company or to obtain illegal benefits. "Weak points" in the information integrity of an enterprise can be used by third parties for gaining access to trade secrets of an enterprise. Information security must be necessarily complex, it must take into account all communication channels and connections between the participants in the accounting process, forsee the implementation of legal, technical, software and organizational measures regulated by the accounting policy of an enterprise.

If the business entity is characterized by the presence of a significant number of employees, the complexity of the management structure, significant volumes of economic activity, a possible option for the formation of separate regulatory documents in cybersecurity with the implementation of information compatibility and unity with accounting policies. An accounting policy in this case can be an integrator of all internal cybersecurity regulations. Thanks to the accounting system, the internal legal field of organization and methods of cybersecurity can be formed, which together comprise the accounting policy of an enterprise.

The information scheme of safety provisions, which are fixed in the internal normative documents and accounting policy, is presented in Fig. 3.1.

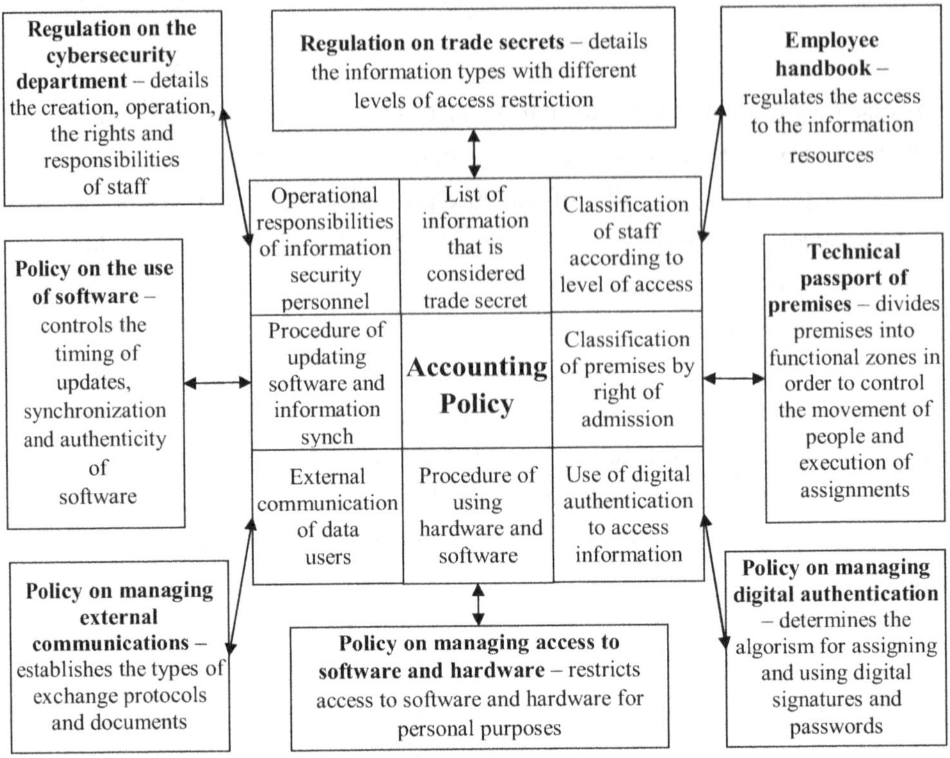

Fig. 3.1. Security regulations in the accounting policy of an enterprise and internal normative documents

The basis of a complex system of information securityat an enterprise is the full distribution of access rights to accounting information. It is advisable for all accounting and administrative employeesdepending on the position and hierarchical level in the management systemto limit physical access to the data base through the mechanism of individual digital signature. With the purpose of ensuring distributed access to accounting information, it is necessary for a company to develop Regulations on trade secrets. According to K.P. Borymska and N.V. Kinzerska, it is necessary to clearly indicate in the Regulations what information is a trade secret, the procedure for classifying them as such, storage conditions, as well as employees of an enterprise who can pass confidential information to representatives of state organizations (Borymska and Kinzerska, 2013).

All personnel of an enterprise must be divided into the level of rights for access. It is advisable to place a table of conformities of each employee to the individual security level in the Regulations on trade secrets. The amount of the given information should be sufficient for performing functional responsibilities or making effective management decisions. The job descriptions of each employee indicate the level of access to trade secrets and the responsibility for its disclosure. As a result, accounting information is limited to accounting and management professionals only in the scope of their direct functional authorities. With the growth of hierarchical level of management,the volume of available accounting information for an acquaintance increases.

It is necessary to indicate in the accounting policy of an enterprise the term of validity of powers in authorised access of employees to trade secrets. The duration of access rights is directly proportional to the level in the management hierarchy. For employees with lower qualifications, it is necessary to significantly reduce the calendar time and access to accounting information. Only with the growth of experience and professional skills it is advisable to increase the level of information trust in a person. Adjustment ofa temporary access to trade secrets will ensure the avoidance of leakage of confidential registration information due to high turnover rate of personnel or temporary employed agents of information malefactors.

With the purpose of preventing unauthorized persons from entering the territory of an enterprise, an automated access system is used. It is recommended to equip all premises of an enterprise with technical tracking devices. Similar to functioning of the system of staff access to accounting information, it is advisable to organize control over the movement of employees throughout an enterprise. The accounting policy should foresee the classification of premises by the right of admission of different groups of employees. Thanks to the system of the automated access mode the control over unauthorized movement of the personnel is provided. It is prohibited for persons to enter premises that do not belong to their direct competence and are not intended for the performance of functional powers.

It is also advisable to control the access of employees to computer and communication equipment. Computer, telecommunications and network systems are owned by the company, which requires its use only for performing work tasks. To prohibit completely the use of software and hardware by the staff for personal goals is quite difficult. It is advisable to determine in the accounting policy the procedure for using the technical and software infrastructure of an enterprise in order to prevent leakage of confidential information through unauthorized information services. Therefore, it is necessary to prohibit access from work computers to certain software, web resources and e-mails that can be used by malefactorsfor violation of the information security of the business entity.

The additional internal regulations must provide a list of all software and hardware in terms of access rights that can be used by the company's staff. In the "Software access control policy" document it is advisable to indicate the following prohibitions: to change and copy files belonging to other users; install third-party software on computers and on the network; send any documents by e-mail to other persons and organizations; to place personal announcements, petitions, advertising offers, etc. It is definitely recommended to mention the possibility of monitoring and verification of the content of all information sent from technical devices and computer programs of the business entityby the company's management.

The distributed access system is implemented through a digital signature mechanism. Each employee is provided with a personal electronic key, which is supplemented by a login and password. The digital key is entered into the employee's software on all technical devices performing functional duties. Personal computers and mobile devices can be used by personnel inside and outside an enterprise. The digital key is exclusively personalized in order to identify each person who is responsible for the implementation of information procedures. Thanks to the system of digital signatures, it is possible to control all information resources and technical devices that the accounting or management specialist dealt with. It is recommended for a company to adopt the Regulations on the use of digital signatures, which regulate the process of assigning and using access keys to accounting information.

The electronic key system is actively used with the purpose of protection and identifying information communications with the country's fiscal service. Therefore, most companies already have sufficient infrastructure to use digital signatures in information processes. It is recommended to supplement the existing system of authentication of officials by obligatory assignment of identified electronic keys to all accounting and management employees. Digital signatures identify the employee in the process of internal and external communications.

For external information links, it is important to specify the selected communication channels. In order to prevent the theft of confidential data, it is important to regulate information flows in the accounting policy of an enterprise. If the communication takes place directly with the counterparty, it is necessary to conclude an agreement with each business entity (institution) on the scheme of organization of information relations. The general conditions of the agreements are synchronized with the accounting policy of an enterprise on the procedure, technology and software and hardware of information exchange. Communication ties with external users through the use of an intermediary operator require connection of a company to common telecommunications channels. The company's management must select and reflect the method of communication in the accounting policy.

As K.P. Borymska and N.V. Kinzerska note, there are special operators on the market that offer a range of services for inter-corporate exchange of electronic information: 1) services for the organization of permanent data exchange – “connection to the network”; 2) services for transfer of accounting information (after connection) – “communication services” (Borymska and Kinzerska, 2013). A distinctive feature of external communication methods is the number of acts of information exchange. When using the method of communication “connection to the network”, the accounting department of an enterprise receives accounting information immediately after it is sent from the sender. In other case (“communication services”), it is recommended to indicate in the accounting policy the time of connection of the software to the communication channels in order to download / unload the accounting information accumulated from the moment of the previous information exchange.

Threatening for information security in automated accounting system can be knavish modifications of special softwear. Computer programs can be modified or they can be substituted by malefactorsfor stealing confidential accounting information. Information protection at an enterprise provides constant control over the authenticity of the software through the mechanism of obtaining and controlling electronic certificates from developers. It is advisable to make an agreement with software manufacturers on the periodic confirmation of the certificate of authenticity. The accounting policy should specify the frequency with which each computer program is inspected for authenticity and integrity. It is obligatory to confirm the electronic certificate by the developer after each update of the program.

Software for the purposes of automation of accounting must be alloted with the following properties: compatibility with other computer programs, prompt correction of errors and corrections without suspending the accounting process, restoration of results in case of software and hardware damage. Special attention from the point of view of protection of accounting information requires the possibility of information synchronization of software products from different manufacturers. With the purpose of organization of free information exchange, it is necessary to specify in the accounting policy of a company the type of a protocol or the format of the exchange file that will be used for synchronization. Determining the type of communication channels when establishing a connection between software will allow to minimize the information threats for the loss of information or theft through the use of unknown exchange protocols. The accounting policy regulates the order of simultaneous use of computer programs, which will not allow accounting and management professionals to make mistakes in the process of performing functional duties.

Similarly, it is necessary to determine the methodology and those responsible for making changes to the algorithm of the software. Accountants with a high level of confidence in trade secrets of an enterprise should be given the right to correct errors and update computer programs in accordance with changes in national legislation or other environmental factors. It is also necessary for an enterprise to determine the order of permanent testing of software products for their relevance and correctness in the accounting policy. At certain intervals, accounting and management professionals need to be instructed how to enter and process the modelled accounting information that has the probabilistic character. In other words, the economic situation in the process of functioning of an enterprise is modeled with the corresponding reflection in the system of accounting and management. After confirming the effectiveness of automated actions, the information is removed from the system in order to avoid the impact on the real economic performance of the entity. There is only a report, which is passed for acquaintance to the management of an enterprise.

3.2. Influence of organizational factors and forms of accounting outsourcing on enterprise cybersecurity

Transformation of socio-economic processes in the shift to digital economy creates unique opportunities for the organization of accounting. Delegation of accounting processes to third parties (outsourcing) is an important optimization method for their organization. Due to the use of computer communication technologies accounting outsourcing has been diversified into several organizational forms. The most popular forms of organizing the delegation of accounting functions include outsourcing by a specialized firm, by an independent accounting expert, by an outstaffer accountant, or by cloud information processing service.

Until recently, the most popular form of accounting outsourcing was the involvement of a specialized outsourcing firm, whose staff performed primary data processing and reporting. Audit firms quite often implement the delegation of accounting functions, which are related to audit services. The social distancing and the remote work of personnel caused by the COVID-19 pandemic make the ability to transfer accounting functions to independent accounting professionals all the more relevant. Such freelance accountants are self-employed and provide outsourcing services on a contractual basis.

Outstaffing is a hybrid form of outsourcing that combines the previous options. Under the terms of an outstaffing contract, accounting specialists who are full-time employees of an independent institution are embedded into the functional structure of the administrative staff of the enterprise. Although outstaffers work for an enterprise that has ordered accounting outsourcing services, they are subordinated to the outsourcing firm. The company providing outstaffing services is responsible for conducting accounting processes. Furthermore, the development of computer communication technologies has led to an increase in cloud delegation of accounting functions. Cloud outsourcing services take on the most time-consuming standard information processing procedures. Given the significant level of automation of computing work, cloud outsourcing is a better option in terms of organizational costs compared to other forms of delegating accounting functions.

Aside from the cost criterion for selecting organizational forms of outsourcing, a set of organizational factors that characterize the methodology and organization of accounting at the enterprise should be distinguished. Variability of organizational factors is the reason for choosing a certain form of outsourcing for each individual business entity, thus minimizing the cyber risks of its operation. In other words, the chosen organizational mode of delegating accounting functions should provide the enterprise with the maximum level of cybersecurity.

The need for cybersecurity of enterprises in terms of outsourcing is given considerable scientific attention. In particular, G. Nassimbeni, M. Sartor and D. Dus investigated the causes and consequences of the risks of outsourcing and offshoring. Assessing the potential risks by analysing failures and their consequences, the researchers argued that cyber threats to enterprise operation are the greatest growing threats to outsourcing and offshoring (Nassimbeni et al., 2012). The most active cyber threats, as M. Benaroch argues, are hazards of IT outsourcing because of the vulnerability of the enterprise information system in the conditions of continuous exchange of information with the outsourcer (Benaroch, 2020). M. Almutairi and S. Riddle proposed to classify cyber risks of IT outsourcing to ensure cybersecurity of enterprises. Based on the improved classification, scientists have developed a methodology for risk management in outsourcing projects (Almutairi and Riddle, 2018). M. Cremonini (2020) continued research on risk management in the context of cybersecurity of outsourced communications, focusing on cloud services delegation of information and functional authority. A. Asatiani et al. emphasize the distinction between cyber risks in terms of cloud and non-cloud outsourcing. Researchers focus on various organizational factors that affect cybersecurity in terms of delegating the processing of accounting information (Asatiani et al., 2019). I. Abdelwahab et al. proposed the concept of minimizing cyber risks based on the use of blockchain technology in order to solve the outlined problems in cybersecurity outsourcing (Abdelwahab et al., 2020).

Delegation of accounting operations in most cases leads to an increase in information threats to the functioning of economic entities. Enterprise management considers the expected benefits of outsourcing, which compensates for potential cyber risks. The need for cybersecurity is also taken into account when assessing the cost-effectiveness of outsourcing. If there is a leak of accounting information that contains a trade secret about certain economic entities or phenomena, it is possible to determine the economic costs the enterprise incurs. Cyber threats may result in possible suspension of economic activity, loss of clients and the market share, non-compliance with the terms of repayment of accounts payable, etc. (Semenyshena et al., 2020). Such consequences should also be taken into account when calculating the cost of managing cyber risks.

Therefore, outsourcing accounting is only possible if the level of cyber threats is acceptable. Cyber threats vary depending on the organizational form of outsourcing, i.e. the delegation of accounting functions, which may engage an outsourcing firm, a third-party accounting specialist, an outstaffer or a cloud information processing service. Accordingly, there is a need to study cyber risks in the context of delegating accounting operations through various organizational forms of outsourcing.

Accounting objectivity – the degree of outsourcing of accounting functions – is the most important organizational factor that affects the cybersecurity of enterprises. Information about the accounting operations transferred to the competence of the outsourcer may be confidential depending on the type of accounting. Delegation of management accounting, given its exclusive functional importance for the purposes of internal information users, may lead to the loss of trade secrets. Instead, outsourcing of financial accounting is accompanied by minimal cyber risks. Data of financial accounting is available to external stakeholders and therefore does not require additional cybersecurity. Thus, the number of accounting functions delegated to the outsourcer directly affects the likelihood of cyber threats.

Similarly, the number of accounting staff determines the risk of outsourcing. If there is only one accountant in the company, delegation of accounting authority is not possible. The larger the accounting staff, the easier it is to outsource accounting, as it involves transferring some operations to third parties. Organization of accounting outsourcing helps to optimize the organizational structure of the enterprise. Outsourcing is applied to the functions of accounting employees who do not operate the trade secrets of the enterprise. Full-time employees can carry out information coordination between the outsourcer and the accounting department of the enterprise.

Work of accounting staff is also associated with the factor of uncertainty, which is explained by the insecurity of the enterprise management in an otherwise effectively functioning accounting system at the enterprise. Insufficient knowledge and professional skills of accounting staff threaten the operation of the entity. First of all, the probability of cyber threats increases with the growing uncertainty associated with the professionalism of accounting staff. Therefore, the delegation of accounting functions is seen as a way to ensure cybersecurity when it comes to the employees who are considered insecure. Similarly, items with a critical level of uncertainty, which can lead to financial and information losses are also subject to delegation.

Remote performance of functional duties by accounting specialists determines the risk of outsourcing, which is explained by the need to optimize and protect communication processes in the enterprise. For example, the exchange of accounting information has already been established for business entities that practice the performance of official duties from home. Accordingly, accounting can be outsourced using already established communication channels, which does not lead to new cyber risks.

The need to ensure business communications with the outsourcer is also an organizational factor that must be taken into account when assessing cyber risks of outsourcing. If the company's accounting staff often provides professional assistance, send and receive accounting information, or update software for an outsourcer, the likelihood of cyber risks increases in the process of electronic communication. Infrequent or non-existent communication with the outsourcer prevents the emergence of significant threats to the cybersecurity of the enterprise.

Supposing accounting functions are delegated to third parties, the need to establish communications with counterparties follows a similar pattern. Outsourcers' access to confidential information about buyers, suppliers, creditors, and other stakeholders threatens the financial and economic activities of the enterprise. Financial and information threats create conditions for possible loss of markets, non-fulfilment of supply contracts, complication of logistics in supply chains, loss of liquidity and solvency of the enterprise, etc.

The level of accounting automation also affects the cybersecurity of the enterprise. On the one hand, comprehensive automation of accounting functions involves the digitization of all business processes, which leads to an increased likelihood of cyber threats of losing large arrays of confidential information during outsourcing. On the other hand, if accounting operations are conducted without the use of computer and communication technologies, the outsourcing becomes significantly more complicated. Delegation of non-automated accounting information processing operations also leads to threats to enterprise cybersecurity due to the need to outsource all business processes.

In this case, the outsourcer gets full access to trade secrets, which maximizes cyber threats. Therefore, the best option for outsourcing accounting is the delegation of those accounting functions that are at least partially automated.

The frequency of information transmissions in the process of accounting also has an impact on enterprise cybersecurity in terms of accounting outsourcing. If accounting information is processed continuously, delegating it to third parties may lead to a breach in security. Accounting outsourcing does not significantly affect cybersecurity in enterprises with low frequency of financial and economic operations and, accordingly, the number of information transmissions (several per day or several per week). Continuous accounting processes, as a rule, remain in the competence of the accounting department of the enterprise. Alternately, periodic information transmissions are more often delegated to outsourcers without significant cyber risks.

The management of the enterprise determines the form of accounting outsourcing that minimizes the likelihood of cyber risks taking into account organizational factors. The analysis presented in Table 3.1 should be used to assess the level of cybersecurity by various organizational factors and forms of outsourcing.

The organizational factors of accounting change depending on the internal and external conditions of operation of economic entities that determine their accounting policy. Table 3.1 reveals the influence of organizational factors (No. 1-8) on the probability of cyber risks for each form of outsourcing (1 - specialized outsourcing firm, 2 - independent accounting expert, 3 - embedded accountant-outstaffer, 4 - cloud information processing service). Each organizational factor has a differentiated effect on the cybersecurity of the enterprise for different forms of outsourcing.

Table 3.1

Assessment of cyber risks probability in terms of accounting organizational factors and forms of accounting outsourcing

Factor No.	Organizational factor / feature of accounting	Form of outsourcing			
		Option 1	Option 2	Option 3	Option 4
		Outsourcing firm	Independent accounting expert	Embedded accountant-outstaffer	Cloud service
1.	- Subject				
	financial accounting	0	0,1	0,2	0
	managerial accounting	0,7	1	1	0,5
2.	- Number of employees				
	1	0,9	0,9	1	0,7
	2-5	0,6	0,7	0,3	0,3
	>6	0,3	0,3	0	0,3
3.	- Uncertainty				
	high	0,2	0,8	0,8	0,2
	moderate	0	0,5	0,5	0,3
	low	0	0,2	0,2	0,2
4.	- Remote work				
	no	0,7	0,7	1	0,9
	yes	0,2	0,2	0,9	0,1
5.	- Communication with the outsourcer				
	no	0	0	0	0
	yes	0,3	0,3	0,3	0,9
6.	- Communication with the stakeholder				
	no	0	0	0	0
	yes	0,7	0,7	0,7	1
7.	- Automation				
	none	1	1	1	0,8
	partial	0,2	0,2	0,2	0,2
	comprehensive	0,6	0,6	0,6	0,2
8.	- Frequency				
	continuous	1	1	1	0,7
	several a day	0,7	0,7	0,7	0,3
	several a week	0,2	0,2	0,2	0,2

The probability of cyber risks is assessed on a scale: 0 - no cyber threats, 0.1-0.3 - cyber threats are unlikely, 0.4-0.7 - cyber threats are moderately likely, 0.8-1 - cyber threats are highly likely.

Source: developed by the author.

For example, the subject of accounting (factor No. 1) is the reason for the increased likelihood of cyber risks for options 2 and 3, due to insufficient reliability of individual accountants-outsourcers in terms of preserving the confidentiality of information. Option 3 has the lowest probability of cyber risks taking into account the number of accounting professionals (factor No. 2) in the outsourcing process. Full-time in-house accountants can monitor the activities of the outstaffer. In addition, the embedded accountants may work with the accounting items that are not related to the trade secret of the enterprise.

"Uncertainty" in accounting (factor No. 3) and related cyber risks is completely eliminated when delegating accounting functions to an outsourcing company due to the involvement of a highly qualified staff of specialists in various fields. On the other hand, engaging the services of one independent or embedded accountant (options 2 and 3) does not have a positive effect on enterprise cybersecurity, as there may be doubts about the qualifications of such accounting professionals.

Established practices of remote work in the performance of accounting functions (factor No. 4) minimizes cyber risks for all forms of outsourcing except when delegating accounting operations to an embedded accountant-outstaffer. Since outstaffing involves the introduction of an outsourcer employee into the company's accounting structure (option 3), making their workstation remote does not minimize cyber risks. Similarly, using cloud information processing services (option 4) differs from other forms of outsourcing in terms of the need for communication with an outsourcer (factor No. 5). As cloud services do not provide comprehensive, multi-faceted professional advice due to the lack of direct communication with accounting professionals, cyber risks increase significantly. The same method is used to assess cyber risks of communications with counterparties (factor No. 6), where option of cloud outsourcing demonstrates the lowest level of cybersecurity as well.

Finally, the degree of automation of accounting work (factor No. 7) and the frequency of accounting data updates (factor No. 8) have almost no effect on enterprise cybersecurity in various forms of outsourcing, as there are uniform cyber risks regardless of the organizational option.

The optimal form of outsourcing for the business entity will be the one with the minimum total probability of cyber risks for all organizational accounting factors. Cyber risks are significantly minimized when delegating accounting functions to cloud services (option 4). However, this option is functionally limited in terms of continuous communications of the outsourcer with the management of the enterprise and stakeholders, which makes it impossible to recommend this form of outsourcing to all entities. Therefore, additional consideration and further research is required on the impact of organizational and legal form, economic sector, size, number of employees of the enterprise on its cybersecurity in terms of accounting outsourcing.

3.3. Combined (integrated) outsourcing of accounting and cybersecurity authorities

The accounting activities of modern enterprises are complicated by numerous organizational constraints. The formation of the digital economy, active hybrid conflicts, the COVID-19 pandemic, the internationalization of markets, the globalization of business communications and other global economic challenges require a transformation of methodology and organization of accounting. Permanent changes in the legislation in the field of accounting and taxation provide for adequate adaptation of accounting practices. Untimely compliance with regulatory requirements can lead to fines and other financial sanctions.

Accounting professionals are required to be multi-skilled and systematically retrained in accordance with changes in socio-economic or legal factors. Updating the knowledge and skills of the company's staff requires the involvement of significant information and financial resources. The probability of suspension of business entities increases with the improvement of accounting policies and the updating of staff skills due to the lack of work in the workplace (inability to remotely perform functional powers), which will lead to a lack of operating income.

To prevent unproductive downtime, the company's management often increases the number of accounting staff. The growth of staff inevitably leads to the actualization of cyber threats to businesses. An effective method of cybersecurity is to limit the access of accounting professionals to certain data sets. The position of the company's management is the need to distribute the functional responsibilities of employees in different objects of accounting with the simultaneous dosing of accounting information. Additionally, the activities of each accounting specialist are monitored by the cybersecurity department. More detailed information on the relationship between accounting and cybersecurity of enterprises is covered in a scientific paper (Zadorozhnyi et al., 2020), which substantiates the priority of information security using accounting techniques for information processing. Thus, management, wanting to minimize financial and information losses, at the same time increases the administrative costs of maintaining an excessively large staff.

The issue of optimizing the costs of dual organization of accounting and security functions is updated. Large businesses often resort to outsourcing services, which involves delegating authority to implement accounting and cybersecurity to third parties. Outsourcing is positioned as a method of optimizing the organizational structure of the enterprise, administrative costs and information risks.

Outsourcing of accounting authority is the subject of research by experts in the field of economics and computer and communication technologies. In particular, Liakhovych G. et al. used the method of SWOT-analysis in the study of different options for outsourcing accounting functions (Liakhovych et al, 2019). The comprehensive transfer of accounting functions to third parties, according to scientists, is inappropriate for most businesses due to significant organizational threats. However, there are no proposals to address the weaknesses of integrated outsourcing. Grigoreva L. explained the mechanism of transformation of methodological and organizational aspects of accounting for outsourcing purposes, which significantly optimizes business processes in the enterprise, omitting the method of information protection of enterprises (Grigoreva, 2019).

However, A. Pylypenko, having improved the design of the contract for the provision of accounting outsourcing services, provides for the need to regulate the procedure for non-disclosure of trade secrets, ranking the levels of access to customer information (Pylypenko, 2019). But the scientist rules out the possibility of simultaneous delegation of accounting and security powers, which is an important means of cyber defense in the context of hybrid conflicts and the development of the digital economy. In fact, while acknowledging the advantages of accounting outsourcing, researchers point out the disadvantages of delegating accounting functions.

Among the disadvantages of accounting outsourcing O. Nazarenko and A. Surovitskaya distinguish the occurrence of costs associated with the transfer of functions to outsourcing; the need to work with only one outsourcer; threat of a raider attack by an outsourcer; the risk of commercial information reaching a competitor (Nazarenko and Surovitskaya, 2018). The list of threats of accounting outsourcing is supplemented by N. Loboda et al., among which are unavailability of accounting database, confidentiality of information, information leakage, loss of efficiency, lack of management accounting (Loboda et al., 2020). T. Maszczak also draws attention to similar threats of outsourcing, but taking into account the size and organizational and legal form of business entities, the number of employees, business profitability, etc. (Maszczak, 2019). However, researchers do not take into account that most organizational constraints are eliminated regardless of the type of business entities through the use of computer and communication technologies in accounting and functional integration of outsourcing theory with other scientific concepts and case studies.

In particular, various scholars have studied the integrative features of accounting in the context of its delegation: T. Martyniuk - functional and information unity of accounting and finance in their outsourcing, which positions the technical requirements for the organization of automated processing of accounting information (Martyniuk, 2016); H. Alkarawy and E. AL-Kuwair - the relationship between accounting outsourcing and management, which contributes to the reengineering of all business processes of the enterprise (Alkarawy and AL-Kuwair, 2021); B. Nicholson and A. Aman - accounting mechanism for the formation of offshore zones, which are based on the delegation of accounting and finance to third parties (Nicholson and Aman, 2012); C. Cullinan and X. Zheng - the interaction of accounting outsourcing and auditing, which reduces the need for audit control due to the optimization of information coordination between participants in the management process in the enterprise (Cullinan and Zheng, 2017); A. Aman Sofiah et al. - the need for financial control over the process of outsourcing accounting functions to justify its feasibility and effectiveness (Sofiah et al, 2013), etc.

To analyze the effectiveness of outsourcing at the stage of post-implementation of the project on the delegation of accounting functions D. Samudrage and D. Jayewardene developed a system of balanced scores. Research on the example of enterprises of different activities has demonstrated the effectiveness and justification of investing in accounting outsourcing (Samudrage and Jayewardene, 2020). However, the potential losses and benefits of information protection were not taken into account when calculating the proposed indicators. On the other hand, there are scientific studies of the security aspects of outsourcing the processing of economic information to third parties (Liu et al, 2017; Stitilis et al, 2020) or cloud services with comprehensive access to accounting databases (Asatiani, 2019) information processes in the economy.

According to the study "The 2019 Kearney Global Services Location Index" (Fig. 3.2), among the surveyed companies the most popular areas of outsourcing are IT services (40.5%), logistics (35.2%) and accounting (32.4 %, of which general accounting functions - 13.5%, payroll accounting - 13.5%, personnel accounting - 5.4%) (Digital resonance: the new factor influencing location attractiveness, 2019).

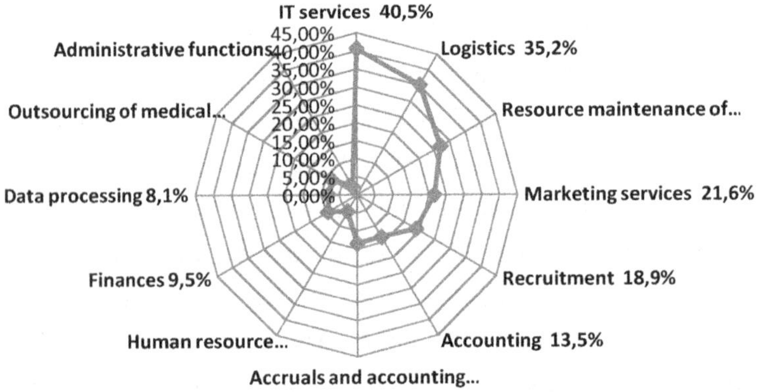

Fig. 3.2. The popularity of outsourcing in terms of delegated business functions

Source: (Zoidze, 2017; Digital resonance: the new factor influencing location attractiveness, 2019)

As it can be seen from Fig. 3.2 some of the surveyed enterprises outsourced in several areas at the same time. Integration of the most popular areas of outsourcing (IT services and accounting) provides synergistic optimization of business processes that are delegated, and minimize enterprise costs. Parallel outsourcing of accounting and security functions helps to minimize information and financial risks of enterprises. Therefore, if the implementation of accounting functions is largely automated and transferred to third parties, it is advisable to delegate the provision of cybersecurity of enterprises. However, the organization of integrated outsourcing of accounting and security powers needs to be clarified, taking into account confidentiality of accounting data, the need to regulate access rights to trade secrets, automation of processing and transmission of information using modern computer and communication technologies. The need to take into account the organizational features of the operation of enterprises to which accounting and security processes are delegated, highlights the need to develop integrated models of outsourcing and determines the purpose of research.

In accounting, information is divided into freely available and confidential. Financial accounting data are made public and passed on to all interested parties upon request, and therefore do not require additional cybersecurity. Financial accounting functions can be fully delegated to third parties. Instead, management records contain trade secrets and are subject to active cyber threats. Confidential information should not leave the information boundaries of the enterprise, which makes it difficult to outsource management accounting. Cybersecurity of such information requires the involvement of cybersecurity professionals and resources at the macro level of the enterprise. For integrated outsourcing of accounting and cybersecurity authorities, it is advisable to use the following organizational models: object, structural, combined (mosaic). The main distinguishing criterion for organizational models of outsourcing is the degree of coverage of accounting and security functions to be delegated in terms of accounting objects and types of accounting or structural units of the enterprise.

According to the first option of outsourcing, financial accounting is fully subject to delegation. It is also advisable to transfer control and cyber protection of financial accounting data that do not contain trade secrets to third parties. However, the implementation of management accounting and its cyber defense should deal with its own accounting and security department of the enterprise. After collection, the primary data should be automatically distributed between the accounting department for management accounting purposes and the consulting firm in a dosed form - financial accounting.

The object field of financial accounting can be further divided into subsets. The most time-consuming aspects of financial accounting in terms of individual accounting objects may be subject to delegation. For example, the accounting of wages or calculations of taxes and fees should be outsourced to minimize the loss of financial resources to repay possible penalties due to incorrect implementation of accounting methods or violations of the law. In this case, the security functions are also distributed in proportion to the delegated accounting authority.

Using the first object model minimizes the cyber risks of the enterprise. The transfer as well as the hypothetical loss of financial accounting data in terms of its delegation does not threaten the cybersecurity of the enterprise. Management accounting and its cyber protection by internal organizational institutions is implemented at the enterprise level, which preventively neutralizes cyber threats.

Under the terms of the second organizational model, it is possible to delegate the functions of financial and management accounting and cybersecurity in terms of individual structural units of the enterprise. In the organizational structure of the enterprise there are centers of responsibility, subsidiaries, territorially separated enterprises, branches, departments that independently implement the requirements of accounting. The use of a structural organizational model involves the delegation of a set of accounting and security powers of the outsourcer in the information framework of a separate business unit. Territorially separated units may lack accounting as an organizational unit due to the full delegation of financial and management accounting to third parties. This type of outsourcing can be done by territorially separated divisions of the enterprise, which operate in the legal field of other states, significantly distinguishing the method of accounting in the parent and subsidiary entities. In this case, the outsourcer eliminates national differences in the organization of accounting.

To minimize cyber risks, it is advisable to consolidate accounting information and its cyber protection in the conditions of outsourcing in the accounting and security department of the enterprise (parent company, central office, administrative department). The integrity of the information model of the business entity is not violated due to point cyber threats. However, additional functions of cybersecurity are entrusted to full-time employees who are obliged to ensure cybersecurity when receiving from separate business units accounting information and its accumulation in the company's accounting. Informational scheme of object and structural organizational model of outsourcing is shown in Fig. 3.3.

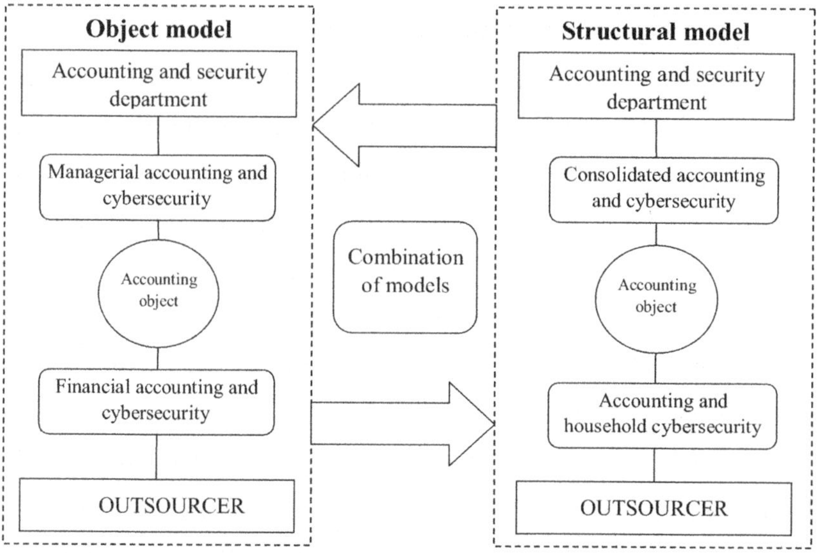

Fig. 3.3. Object and structural organizational model of outsourcing
Source: developed by the authors

Thus, the object and structural organizational models of outsourcing involve the dual implementation of accounting functions in accordance with the company's accounting and third parties. The increase in the amount of delegated authority for the processing of credentials and their cyber protection allows for the loss of confidential information and information fraud or malicious manipulation. Therefore, the complex transfer of accounting and security powers to an outsourcer is complicated due to the manifestation of significant cyber risks.

To ensure effective cyber protection and avoid organizational constraints on the implementation of object and structural outsourcing options, it is advisable to use a combined (mosaic) model. The main idea of the proposed organizational model is to combine the features of object and structural options of outsourcing with a mosaic delegation of accounting and security functions to many outsourcers. All accounting and cybersecurity tasks are divided into several subsets, which are transferred to different third parties.

The primary element of automated accounting can be a system of technological sensors that operate on the principles of Internet of Things technology. Technological devices for collecting credentials operating on the principles of Internet of Things technology can be equipment for the following purposes: robotic production, radio frequency identification of material values, employee biometrics, verification of payment for services, electronic money transactions, GPS navigation of transport (Shevchuk et al., 2020) etc. Credentials collected automatically using the Internet of Things are immediately sent over a global network to places where they are processed or stored. Technological sensors work autonomously without the direct participation of accounting professionals, which minimizes financial and cyber risks. Accounting staff do not have full access to information at the stage of its collection, respectively, malicious information manipulations are prevented. There is a need to ensure control over the functioning of accounting and management staff in the subsequent stages of information processing for the purposes of its cybersecurity.

The primary data collected using the Internet of Things technology is subject to clustering, accumulation and transfer to users for further processing. Classified credentials are broadcast to stakeholders (including outsourcers) to a limited extent in accordance with access rights and functional responsibilities. Information communications take place exclusively in electronic form on the principles of distance. Outsourcers can be at a considerable territorial distance from the places of primary data generation. Due to the lack of spatial constraints, the number of outsourcers involved in the implementation of accounting and security powers may be unlimited. Additionally, some of the functions of automatic processing of accounting information are performed by cloud services. Involving a significant number of participants in the information process requires the use of effective communication mechanisms and network technologies.

The fundamental basis of the combined (mosaic) version of outsourcing is to choose blockchain network technology, which combines accounting fragments into a single information model of enterprise operation. It is advisable to delegate financial and management accounting in terms of their facilities to another company that provides outsourcing services. It is also not recommended to outsource the accounting and cybersecurity features of a particular account to a single outsourcing firm. For example, accounting and cybersecurity of information about the costs of the enterprise must be carried out by various outsourcers. Separate delegation of accounting and security functions reduces the likelihood of cyber threats and the loss of critically large data sets, which threatens the functioning of enterprises. The information scheme of the combined (mosaic) organizational model of outsourcing is shown in Fig. 3.4.

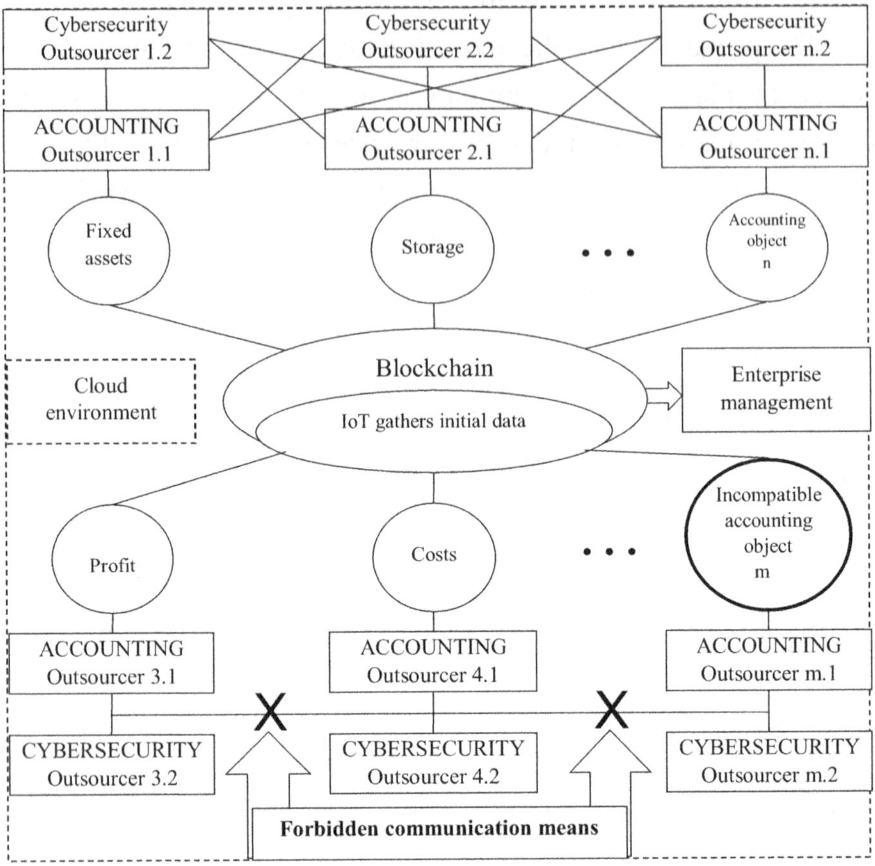

Fig. 3.4. Combined (mosaic) version of outsourcing
Source: developed by the authors

It is critical to differentiate the accounting information that reaches one outsourcer for certain accounting objects. For example, it is impractical to simultaneously delegate the authority to account for income and expenses to a third party, which may result in the loss of information about the company's profits or losses.

The division of the information field of the enterprise can be carried out on more detailed sets. It is advisable for various outsourcers to submit for processing accounting information about a particular object of accounting in the context of different time periods, business units, enterprises' employees, production processes, etc. With the help of blockchain technology, disparate accounting information is integrated and transmitted to the accounting and management of the enterprise for further processing. Each outsourcer operates exclusively with mosaic data sets required for the implementation of partial accounting or security functions.

CONCLUSIONS

1. The increasing number of cyberattacks as part of the hybrid influence on social and economic processes and the threat of confidential information leaks dictate the need to ensure cybersecurity for enterprises, sectors and branches of the economy. The accounting system should be used as the basis for ensuring the cybersecurity of enterprises since much of the accounting information is confidential, modern accounting specialists are qualified in multiple different areas of expertise, numerous cyberattacks are perpetrated via accounting software, and internal regulations document information processes. Effective cybersecurity requires the enterprise to review the operational responsibilities of accounting specialists so that they acquire additional skills and abilities, document their responsibilities in the employee handbooks, establishing liability for violating cybersecurity, and improve internal and external regulations that pertain to information and security processes.

The main regulation documenting the method of processing and protecting information is the accounting policy of the enterprise. The accounting policy or additional derivative internal regulations should determine the procedure for identifying trade secrets, managing access to information with digital authentication, using software and hardware in order to automate accounting and management, external communication with the stakeholders, and the security of physical and information networks of the enterprise. Additionally, the accounting policy should provide for the creation of the security audit service or the involvement of independent external auditors from consulting and auditing firms to monitor the cybersecurity of the enterprise. Conducting security audits helps to better prepare the management of the enterprise detect cyber threats by developing efficient ways to predict, prevent and eliminate them.

2. Activization of cyber threats requires development of effective methods of cyber defense. In order to unify the means of cybersecurity of enterprises, it is necessary to focus on single fundamental principles of cybersecurity of accounting information. The main principle in the secured value of accounting information is its reliability. Reliability of accounting information indicates the absence of errors, distortions, inaccuracies caused by third parties, as well as it guarantees availability and confidentiality.

The principles of confidentiality, integrity and accessibility are connected with the reliability of records. Adherence to these principles ensures that high-quality accounting information reaches internal and external stakeholders without losing the company's trade secrets. The theoretical foundation of cybersecurity of accounting information is supplemented by the principles of completeness, sanction, adressness, reliability and comparability. These principles are the basis for the development of guidelines for cybersecurity of enterprises to prevent, avoid and eliminate the consequences of threats to the security of accounting information. Very important for obtaining reliable accounting information is adherenceof the theoretical principles of accounting and computer science. However, with the further improvement of computer and communication technologies and the evolutionary complication of cyber threats to the functioning of enterprises, it is possible to supplement the list of fundamental principles of cyber protection of accounting information.

3. The need for effective cybersecurity of accounting data requires adaptive consideration of various cyber threats. The type of cyber risks can determine the significant differences in measures to prevent, avoid and eliminate potential consequences. Therefore, it is advisable to group the cyber risks of accounting data using the classification criteria of intent, mode, information and financial interest, location, instigator, origin, goal,

target, scale, form of manifestation, legality, aspect, duration, latency, probability, and consequences.

Classification by other criteria related to the activities of criminals or stakeholders is not very informative for the purposes of protection against cyber threats. The increasing complexity of information processes and advancements in computer and communication technologies precipitate the need for improvements in the suggested classification of cyber threats to accounting data, and therefore, further scientific research.

4. The implementation of computer and communication technologies in all socio-economic processes has led to the growing number and intensity of cyber threats to enterprise operation. The ultimate goal of cyber threats is to obtain economic benefits for third parties or to cause economic damage to businesses. There is a direct relationship between cyber risks and the economic condition of the enterprise.

Accounting should be considered an innovative mechanism of ensuring the interaction between the economic and cybersecurity of the enterprise. Accounting links are present at five accumulative levels and explain the impact of cyber risk activity on the increase in threats to the economic security of economic entities. At the methodological level, the cyber threats concern the principles and functions of accounting; at the quality level – the quality of accounting data; at the methodical level – accounting items and types; at the communication level – accounting communications with stakeholders; at the reputation level – business image of the enterprise, which leads to economic losses for the enterprise. At the same time, the accounting methods create the conditions for the feedback between economic and cybersecurity, which consists of reliable identification and assessment of economic losses from the manifestation of cyber risks.

5. Activation of cyber threats due to global hybrid conflicts, COVID-19 pandemic, economic imbalances, requires the organization of an effective system of enterprises' cyberdefense. The main object of cyber-

attacks in digital economy is accounting information. Cyber threats are manifested at all stages of processing of accounting information and its transmission to users (stakeholders).For developing effective measures to minimize cyber threats, it is necessary to understand their impact on the functioning of stakeholders in terms of their various types.

The traditional classification of accounting information users is irrelevant for the purposes of enterprises cybersecurity, as it does not take into account the activation of variable cyber threats that requires improving the classification of stakeholders. Users of accounting information should be classified according to the criteria: the ability to manage the activities of the business entity, the right of access, the likelihood of cyber threats, the ability to dispose of access rights, access to accounting objects, functional law, information processing, economic activity, age of individuals, organizational and legal form of legal entities, type of used communication channels, frequency of information acts.

6. Traditional electronic document management in accounting has a number of functional limitations, which is the cause of cybersecurity vulnerabilities of enterprises. To implement effective internal and external electronic communications, it is advisable to implement blockchain technology in document management, which meets modern requirements for cybersecurity of enterprises. The fact of collecting primary data initiates the start of further information processes of processing and distribution of accounting information. Documented data using blockchain technology is fragmented, encrypted and sent in dosed form to internal and external users in accordance with the information needs and access rights to trade secrets. The permissive mode of accounting information processing should be implemented using a system of digital signatures and cloud placement of distributed databases.

The use of blockchain technology in electronic documentation and document management provides: fragmentation, complementarity, scalability, duplication, chronology, confidentiality, distribution, accessibility, openness of accounting information processing, which is the basis for effective cybersecurity of the enterprise. The organization of cybersecurity in the conditions of distributed structuring of the accounting information promotes openness of document circulation at the enterprise that reduces need for application of isolating information practices. The openness of information exchange using blockchain technology for cybersecurity of information minimizes organizational constraints in the formation of the digital economy and creates favorable conditions for the progressive innovative development of social formation.

7. The need to obtain prompt access to funds through electronic communications, protecting investment after the global financial crisis has led to the emergence of a new type of electronic money – the cryptocurrencies. Cryptocurrencies gain significant popularity due to the advantages of their use, such as: comfort, independence, accessibility, lack of engagement, confidentiality, no documents, full automation of accounting, and cost optimization.

Cash as a means of money turnover is losing popularity progressively in commercial settlements that allows to refuse such organizational structure as a cashier and with that, from documents and accounting professionals responsible for cash transactions. The possibility of integrated support of personal wallets for electronic money in mobile devices provides non-cash settlement for purchased goods (services) similar to bank cards.

Evolutionary development of electronic money, international payment systems, information systems of remote notification and fund management requires adequate changes in the organization and methods of automated management accounting of non-cash transactions. Modern systems of remote management of the "Client-Bank" and "Internet-Bank" accounts are characterized by certain organizational constraints that do not meet the modern notions of non-cash transactions with help of the cryptocurrencies and other electronic money. Combining the functional capabilities of the blockchain technology, positive qualities of the communications "Internet Bank" and "Client-Bank" will allow to create a hybrid system of non-cash payments by cryptocurrencies, electronic money, funds on accounts in a bank with free conversion of existing funds and opportunities for information exchange with all the participants in settlement operations. Collection of accounting information on settlements with the cryptocurrencies and other electronic money is carried out without formation of the traditional payment documents and bank statements. Electronic information from the hybrid communication system is the foundation for providing cybersecurity, fully automated documenting, formation of accounting records, informing accountants and management of non-cash transfers. Automation of accounting of cash transactions helps to increase the level of cyber defense control over execution of money transactions due to timely and remote informing sharing about the parameters of non-cash payments.

8. Areas of IoT using in the accounting automation and enterprise cybersecurity are: the transformation of accounting, improving the audit control of economic activity and optimization of accounting and control specialists work. The use of IoT devices provides: reducing the participation of the human factor in the processing of accounting information, distancing the capturing and processing of primary data, automation of business documentation, delegation of accounting and security authorities, compliance with quality information and improving the form of accounting for Big data ready.

Along with the significant advantages of the implementation of IoT technology in the activities of enterprises there are disadvantages - active cyber risks. Threats to entities cybersecurity are: theft, substitution and blocking of information, gaining control over the equipment or denial of its operation, increasing the access rights of employees and outsiders to enter the prohibited territorial information boundaries of the enterprise. Prevention and avoidance of cyber threats IoT devices using requires regulation of communication channels of credentials, regulation of access rights to confidential data, use of a policy of permanent password renewal for access to databases and technology sensors, correct distribution of information flows between different stakeholders. Therefore, the risks of implementing IoT technology are significantly minimized provided the effective organization of accounting with its positioning as a basis for establishing cybersecurity of information flows.

9. To ensure control over the access of employees to information and material flows, automated checkpoint systems are used to admit employees to the premises and buildings of the enterprise. The operation of the system mainly involves the implementation of security functions. However, modern conditions of growing cyber threats caused by the hybrid conflicts around the world and looming biological threat of the COVID-19 pandemic necessitate the introduction of biometric authentication of employees, leading to the transformation in the accounting and control over time worked by the employees, accrual of basic and additional wages, as well as creation of digital primary documents and reports consequently sent to stakeholders.

Biometric employee authentication should be used when they cross between separate functional areas of the enterprise and its individual buildings. The entire territory of the entity should be divided into different functional areas for different groups of staff in order to restrict access to confidential information, which will help ensure a sufficient level of cybersecurity of the enterprise. It is recommended to pay wages in accordance with the time spent within the areas that correspond to the functional duties of the employee or the time spent operating equipment connected to their official duties (including from home). For the purposes of automated accounting and control, functional and time regulations for the implementation of functional responsibilities and stay in certain types of premises are developed in advance for each employee. Regulating the time parameters of employees' work helps to avoid overcrowding on the premises of the enterprise, which helps to minimize biological threats (COVID-19 infection).

It is advisable to introduce one minute as the measure unit to ensure effective accounting and control of the time worked. The use of a more detailed unit of measure creates an opportunity to account for and control deviations from the standards of working time, ensure self-management of employees, and increase their productivity. Failure to comply with the work schedule may be grounds for review of working conditions or the need for professional retraining of the relevant specialist. On the other hand, information on overtime work (including remote performance of official duties from home) should lead to the accrual of additional compensation and incentive payments to employees.

Information from the system of biometric employee authentication on the performance of functional duties at the employees' workstations at home or work can be used to help optimize the accounting of employee costs. Automation can also be used in accounting for the cost of food, operation of common areas, overhead costs with a clear distribution between production, administrative, marketing and other costs. Information on time worked and wages created by the system of biometric employee authentication is summarised in electronic form and sent to internal and external stakeholders.

10. The progressive development of communication technologies creates new requirements for data transfer speeds. The use of 4G cellular communication and the new generation of 5G is not able to meet the information needs of users of artificial intelligence technologies, total virtualization of communications, unmanned and autopilot vehicles, connection to the Internet of all technical devices, which requires the concept of 6G mobile communications.

An important advantage of the sixth generation of cellular communication is the three-dimensional reliable determination of the subscriber's location and direct information connection between the elements of the cellular network, which allows transformation of accounting of enterprises in various fields. In particular, fundamental changes are made to the accounting of costs with the use of: production equipment connected to the information system of an enterprise, for permanent timely determination of the cost of industrial products; vehicles with controlled movement by agreed routes and preventive identification of the cost of providing transport services; swarms of unmanned aerial vehicles for aerovisual observation of agricultural and construction works with reliable definition and distribution of income and expenses; technologies for counting the number of visitors to the company's premises to determine the popularity of retail space and advertising in order to inform customers about their value.

At the same time, the information system of enterprises using 6G cellular networks is threatened by significant cyber risks: attacks using artificial intelligence, previously unknown vulnerabilities of "Zero Day", risks based on quantum calculations, attacks using fast (TeraHertz) equipment, hybrid wars etc. To ensure cybersecurity, it is necessary to use 6G cellular networks to monitor: the location of employees on the territory or premises of an enterprise; routes of movement and performance of works by vehicles; access of persons to production equipment, construction sites or places of agricultural work; the presence of criminals at the scene of offenses in order to prevent the loss of material and information resources of economic entities.

11. In the accounting policy of an enterprise or in separate internal regulations it is offered to fix: the list of the information which is a trade secret; the procedure for updating software and methods of information synchronization with cloud services; implementation of external communications with users of information; the procedure for using software and hardware; algorithm of distribution and application of electronic keys for access to information; classification of premises by the right of admission and organization of the system of protection of the

territory of an enterprise; classification of employees according to the hierarchical level of access to information resources of an enterprise, etc.

Information protection in conditions of automation of accounting and management involves a combination of organizational actions of employees of an enterprise, which should be reflected in the accounting policy and internal regulations. The security provisions of the regulation of processing of accounting data require establishment of an effective division of functional powers of staff and granting of access rights to confidential information. Access to databases is realized through the issuance of personal digital signatures, logins and passwords. Thanks to the technologies of authorization, the responsibility and track of the staff's actions concerning data processing and transmission is established.

Through reflecting the time criteria for conducting checks of the state of information security, data exchange protocols, exchange types of documents, certificates and licenses for the use of software at an enterprise, the reliability of accounting information in the process of performing functional and accounting responsibilities by accounting and management specialists is guaranteed.

12. Shift to digital economy, growing number of global hybrid threats, and remote processing of information caused by the COVID-19 pandemic necessitate accounting to be improved. One of the methods for optimizing accounting is the delegation of accounting functions (outsourcing). Transfer of accounting information and functions is accompanied by active cyber threats. Under conditions of outsourcing accounting, it is necessary to identify cyber risks in terms of variable accounting factors to ensure the enterprise cybersecurity.

The organizational factors of accounting that affect the cybersecurity of enterprises include the subject of accounting, number of employees, uncertainty, remote work, communication with the outsourcer, communication with stakeholders, automation, frequency of information updates. According to the selected organizational options, it is possible to assess the probability of cyber risks in terms of different forms of accounting outsourcing.

Cyber risks are significantly minimized when delegating accounting operations to cloud information-processing services. However, the cloud version of delegation is complicated if there is need for continuous communication of the outsourcer with the management of the company and stakeholders, which make it impossible to recommend such an option of outsourcing for all businesses. Therefore, the optimal form of outsourcing for each business entity is the one with the minimum total probability of cyber risks for all organizational accounting factors.

13. Integrated positioning of accounting and security authority outsourcing is necessary to optimize the functioning of enterprises. Combined delegation of accounting and cybersecurity functions will help synergistically minimize administrative costs, reduce the likelihood of information and financial risks. The integration of outsourcing is possible in two ways, depending on the objects and types of accounting (object model) or the organizational structure of the enterprise (structural model).

The implementation of the object model involves the delegation of processing and cybersecurity of financial accounting information about individual objects of accounting. Operation of management accounting information, which may contain trade secrets, is performed only in the accounting department of the enterprise. According to the structural organizational model, outsourcing of accounting and security powers is possible only for the operation of business units of the enterprise (structural units) with the consolidation of information in the accounting of the parent company. Due to the manifestation of significant cyber risks, a comprehensive delegation of all accounting and security powers in the object and structural model of outsourcing is impossible.

To avoid organizational constraints on the implementation of object and structural options for outsourcing, it is advisable to use a combined (mosaic) model, which is a mosaic delegation of accounting and security functions to many outsourcers. All accounting and cybersecurity powers are divided into subsets and delegated to various outsourcers, which are informationally combined using blockchain technology. With the help of blockchain technology, disparate accounting information is integrated and transmitted to the accounting and management of the enterprise for further processing. The implementation of the proposed model provides comprehensive outsourcing of accounting and security functions with an effective system of cybersecurity of enterprises.

REFERENCES

1. 2019 Cyberthreat Defense Report (2019). CyberEdge Group. Annapolis: CyberEdge Group. 50 p.

2. Abdelwahab, I., Ramadan, N. & Hefny, H. (2020). Cybersecurity Risks of Blockchain Technology. International Journal of Computer Applications. 177. 8-14. 10.5120/ijca2020919922.

3. Aisenberg, Michael & Editor, Esq. (2018). State and Local ICT Policy: A Framework for Cybersecurity, IOT, Cloud, Block Chain, etc. Sub-Federal Cyber Policy. URL: https://www.researchgate.net/publication/334747029_State_and_Local_ICT_Policy_A_Framework_for_Cybersecurity_IOT_Cloud_Block_Chain_etc.

4. Aleksandrov, I.A, Polovian, O.V. (2000) Klasteryzatsiia terytorialnykh utvoren Ukrainy za rivnem ekonomichnoi bezpeky [Clustering of territorial formations of Ukraine by the level of economic security]. Ekonomichna kibernetyka – Economic Cybernetics. № 5-6. 40-47.

5. Alibhai, Salim, Bakker, Erwin, Balasubramanian, T., Bharadva, Kunal, Chaudhry, Asif, Coetsee, Danie, Johnstone, Chris, Kuria, Patrick, Naidoo, Christopher & Ramanarayanan, J. (2021). Accounting policies, changes in accounting estimates and errors. Interpretation and Application of IFRS® Standards. Wiley. 117-137. 10.1002/9781119818663.ch7.

6. Alkarawy, H. & AL-Kuwair, E. (2021). Accounting improving the costs and business process management in transportation to a third party. Accounting. 701-708. 10.5267/j.ac.2020.12.006.

7. Al-Mohammed, H. & Yaacoub, E. (2021). On The Use of Quantum Communications for Securing IoT Devices in the 6G Era. 1-6. 10.1109/ICCWorkshops50388.2021.9473793.

8. Almutairi, M. & Riddle, S. (2018). A Framework for Managing Security Risks of Outsourced IT Projects. An Empirical Study. 40-44. 10.1145/3178461.3178476.

9. Alsaqa Zeyad, H., Hussein, A. I., Mohammed Mahmood, S. (2020). The Impact of Blockchain on Accounting Information Systems. Journal of Information Technology Management, 11. 62-80. 10.22059/jitm.2019.74301.

10. Asatiani, A., Apte, U., Penttinen, E., Rönkkö, M. & Saarinen, T. (2019). Impact of accounting process characteristics on accounting outsourcing - Comparison of users and non-users of cloud-based accounting information systems. International Journal of Accounting Information Systems. 34. 10.1016/j.accinf.2019.06.002.

11. Asieieva, Yu. (2020). Problem questions of cyber-addictions classification. Psychology and Personality. 2. 23-40. 10.33989/2226-4078.2020.2.211910.

12. Avtomatyzovana systema kontroliu dostupu [Automated access control system]. Material z Vikipedii – vilnoi entsyklopedii – From Wikipedia, the free encyclopedia. URL: https://uk.wikipedia.org/wiki/Автоматизована_система_контролю_доступу.

13. B2B cross-border transactions on blockchain in various regions worldwide in 2020 with forecasts from 2021 to 2025. Statista. https://www.statista.com/statistics/1228825/b2b-cross-border-transactions-on-blockchain-worldwide/

14. Badhwar, Raj. (2021). AI for Cybersecurity. The CISO's Next Frontier. 41-44. 10.1007/978-3-030-75354-2_4.

15. Balaziuk, O.Yu., Sysoieva, I.M., Pilyavets, V.M. (2020). Control and accounting aspects of introducing agile methodology for software development projects. Financial and credit activity: problems of theory and practice. 3 (34). 94-102.

16. Bansal, S.K., Batra, R., Jain, N. (2018). Blockchain and the future of accounting, The Management Accountant Journal, No. 6, 60-66.

17. Baranenko, R.V. (2021). Cyber attacks as a form of cyber terrorism. Scientific notes of Taurida National V.I. Vernadsky University. Series: Technical Sciences. 1. 45-50. 10.32838/2663-5941/2021.1-1/07.

18. Benaroch, M. (2020). Cybersecurity Risk in IT Outsourcing—Challenges and Emerging Realities. Information Systems Outsourcing. 313-334. 10.1007/978-3-030-45819-5_13.

19. Biometriia [Biometrics]. Material z Vikipedii – vilnoi entsyklopedii – From Wikipedia, the free encyclopedia. URL: https://uk.wikipedia.org/wiki/Біометрія.

20. Bonson, E., Bednarova, M. (2019). Blockchain and its implications for accounting and auditing, Meditari Accountancy Research, Vol. 27 No. 5, 725-740. 10.1108/MEDAR-11-2018-0406.

21. Boonkrong, S. (2021). Biometric Authentication. Authentication and Access Control, 107-132. doi: 10.1007/978-1-4842-6570-3_5.

22. Borymska, K. P. (2013). Zakhyst bukhhalterskoi informatsii v oblikovii politytsi z metoiu opodatkuvannia: orhanizatsiini aspekty [Protection of accounting information in accounting policy for tax purposes: organizational aspects]. Zbirnyk naukovykh prats Natsionalnoho universytetu derzhavnoi podatkovoi sluzhby Ukrainy. – Collection of scientific works of the National University of the State Tax Service of Ukraine. 2013. № 2. 14-21. URL: http://nbuv.gov.ua/UJRN/znpnudps_2013_2_4.

23. Borymska, K.P. and Kinzerska, N.V. (2013) Kontseptualizatsiia zakhystu bukhhalterskoi informatsii pry mizhkorporatyvnomu elektronnomu dokumentooboroti torhovelnykh pidpryiemstv: problemni aspekty [Conceptualization of the protection of accounting information in the inter-corporate electronic document circulation of trade enterprises: problem aspects], Bulletin of ZHSTU – Visnyk ZHDTU, 3 (65), 16-25.

24. Bukhhalterskyi oblik v upravlinni pidpryiemstvom [Accounting in enterprise management] (2017). / O.A. Lahovska, S.F. Lehenchuk, V.I. Kuz, S.V. Kucher. Zhytomyr: Zhytomyrskyi derzhavnyi tekhnolohichnyi universytet. 416 p. URL: https://learn.ztu.edu.ua/mod/resource/view.php?id=17967.

25. Cai, C.W. (2021). Triple-entry accounting with blockchain: how far have we come?, Accounting Finance. 10.1111/acfi.12556.

26. Chesney, Steve, Roy, Kaushik & Khorsandroo, Sajad. (2021). Machine Learning Algorithms for Preventing IoT Cybersecurity Attacks. 10.1007/978-3-030-55190-2_53.

27. Chikutuma, C. (2016). Integrated Reporting: A Story of Stakeholder Accountability. 5th International Conference on Accounting, Auditing, and Taxation (ICAAT 2016). 10.2991/icaat-16.2016.4.

28. Chukhno, I. S. (2012). Udoskonalennia klasyfikatsii korystuvachiv zvitnosti [Improving the classification of reporting users]. Oblik i finansy. – Accounting and finance. № 1. 85-90. URL: http://nbuv.gov.ua/UJRN/Oif_apk_2012_1_17.

29. Cohen, E. E. (2018). IoT for auditors and accountants; auditing the IoT. Retrieved from https://www.unece.org/fileadmin/DAM/cefact/cf_forums/2018_Geneva/PPTs/IoT_PPTs/12_-_Eric_Cohen_-_IoT_CEFACT.pdf.

30. Coyne, J.G., McMickle, P.L. (2017). Can Blockchains serve an accounting purpose, Journal of Emerging Technologies in Accounting, Vol. 14 No. 2, 101-111, 10.2308/jeta-51910.

31. Cremonini, M. (2020). Cloud Security Risk Management. Cloud Computing Security. 95-114. 10.1201/9780429055126-10.

32. Cullinan, C. & Zheng, X. (2017). Accounting outsourcing and audit lag. Managerial Auditing Journal. 32. 276-294. 10.1108/MAJ-03-2016-1349.

33. Demirkan, Sebahattin, Demirkan, Irem & Mckee, Andrew. (2020). Blockchain technology in the future of business cybersecurity. Journal of Management Analytics. Vol. 7, Issue 2. 189-208. DOI: 10.1080/23270012.2020.1731721.

34. Denha S.M and Veryha Yu.O. (2004). Zakhyst informatsii v komp`yuternykh informatsiinykh systemakh bukhhalterskoho obliku [Protection of information in computer information systems accounting]. Bukhhalterskyi oblik i audyt - Accounting and auditing. 5, 59-65.

35. Denha, S. M., Veryha, Yu. O. (2004). Zakhyst informatsii v komp`yuternykh informatsiinykh systemakh bukhhalterskoho obliku [Information protection in computer information systems of accounting]. Bukhhalterskyi oblik i audyt – Accounting and auditing. 5. 59-65.

36. Desyatnyuk O., Muravskyi V. and Shevchuk O. (2021). Accounting Automation in Agroindustrial Enterprises Using Drones (UAVs). 11th International Conference on Advanced Computer Information Technologies (ACIT). 337-341. https://doi.org/10.1109/ACIT52158.2021.9548424.

37. Digital resonance: the new factor influencing location attractiveness (2019). The 2019 Kearney Global Services Location Index. URL: https://www.kearney.com/digital-transformation/gsli/2019-full-report.

38. Djenna, Amir, Saidouni, Djamel Eddine & Wafia, Abada. (2020). A Pragmatic Cybersecurity Strategies for Combating IoT-Cyberattacks. 1-6. 10.1109/ISNCC49221.2020.9297251.

39. Drokina, N. & Kaipova, Gulnara. (2020). Formation of accounting policy content. Chronos Journal. 10.31618/2658-7556-2020-40-1-3.

40. Dupuis, Marc & Renaud, Karen. (2020). Scoping the ethical principles of cybersecurity fear appeals. Ethics and Information Technology. 1-20. 10.1007/s10676-020-09560-0.

41. Dykyi, A.P., Semenchuk, M.V. (2005). Komertsiina taiemnytsia yak skladova ekonomichnoi bezpeky pidpryiemstva [Trade secret as a component of economic security of the enterprise]. Visnyk Zhytomyrskoho derzhavnoho tekhnolohichnoho universytetu. Ekonomichni nauky – Bulletin of Zhytomyr State Technological University. Economic sciences. № 4 (34). 75-82.

42. Eaton, Tim, Grenier, Jonathan & Layman, David. (2019) Accounting and Cybersecurity Risk Management. Current Issues in Auditing. Vol. 13, No. 2, C1-C9. DOI: 10.2308/ciia-52419.

43. El-Ebiary, Y. & Alawi, N. (2020). The Risks of Accounting Information Systems. International Journal of Engineering Trends and Technology. 2231-2381. 10.14445/22315381/CATI3P220.

44. Estimate of overall cryptocurrency market cap per week from July 2010 to June 2021. Statista. https://www.statista.com/statistics/730876/cryptocurrency-maket-value/

45. Fletcher, J., Gillum, D., Moritz, R., & Schwartz, A. (2020). Demographic and Salary Trends of the 2020 Biosafety Workforce. Applied Biosafety, 3. doi: 10.1089/apb.20.0066.

46. Fubara-Manuel, I. (2020). Biometric Capture. African Diaspora, 12, 1-25. doi: 10.1163/18725465-01201002.

47. Global 5G subscription forecast 2019-2025. Statista. https://www.statista.com/statistics/760275/5g-mobile-subscriptions-worldwide/

48. Global Biometrics in Workforce Management Market 2019. Data Snapshot: Biometrics in the workplace commonplace, but are they secure? URL: https://community.spiceworks.com/security/articles/2952-data-snapshot-biometrics-in-the-workplace-commonplace-but-are-they-secure.

49. Global Connectivity Index – GCI Ranking Table. https://www.huawei.com/minisite/gci/en/country-rankings.html.

50. Global Cybersecurity Index (GCI) 2018. (2019) / International Telecommunication Union. Geneva : ITUPublications. 86 p. https://www.itu.int/dms_pub/itu-d/opb/str/D-STR-GCI.01-2018-PDF-E.pdf.

51. Global Innovation Index 2018. https://www.wipo.int/edocs/pubdocs/en/wipo_pub_gii_2018-intro5.pdf.

52. Gomaa, A.A., Gomaa, M.I., Stampone, A. (2019). A transaction on the Blockchain: an AIS perspective, intro case to explain transactions on the ERP and the role of the internal and external auditor, Journal of Emerging Technologies in Accounting, Vol. 16 No. 1, 47-64, 10.2308/jeta-52412.

53. Grigoreva, L. (2019). Accounting Outsourcing: Theoretical Bases and Methodological Provision. Vestnik NSUEM. 143-154. 10.34020/2073-6495-2019-2-143-154.

54. Gupta, W. (2020). Salary Estimator using Data Science. International Journal for Modern Trends in Science and Technology, 6, 319-322. 10.46501/IJMTST061259.

55. Haapamäki, Elina & Sihvonen, Jukka (2019). Cybersecurity in accounting research. Managerial Auditing Journal. No. 34. 808-834. DOI: 10.1108/MAJ-09-2018-2004.

56. Haque, Md, Haque, Shameemul, Kumar, Kailash & Singh, Narendra. (2021). A Comprehensive Study of Cybersecurity Attacks, Classification, and Countermeasures in the Internet of Things. 63-90. 10.4018/978-1-7998-4201-9.ch004.

57. Harrast, Steven. (2020). Robotic process automation in accounting systems. Journal of Corporate Accounting & Finance. 31. 4. 10.1002/jcaf.22457.

58. Henry Matey, Akwetey, Danquah, Paul, Koi-Akrofi, Godfred & Asampana, Isaac. (2021). Critical Infrastructure Cybersecurity Challenges: IoT in Perspective. International Journal of Network Security & Its Applications. 13. 41-58. 10.5121/ijnsa.2021.13404.

59. Hentea, Mariana. (2021). Principles of Cybersecurity. Building an Effective Security Program for Distributed Energy Resources and Systems: Understanding Security for Smart Grid and Distributed Energy Resources and Systems, 93-127. 10.1002/9781119070740.ch3.

60. Herasymovych, I. (2018). Orhanizatsiia oblikovoi polityky suchasnoho pidpryiemstva [Organization of accounting policies of the modern enterprise]. Investytsiyi: praktyka ta dosvid, 7, 49-53.

61. Honcharuk, M.O. (2012). Kompiuteryzatsiia bukhhalterskoho obliku bezghotivkovykh rozrakhunkiv [Computerization of non-cash accounting]. Problemy teorii ta metodolohii bukhhalterskoho obliku, kontroliu i analizu – Problems of the theory and methodology of accounting, control and analysis, Issue. 2 (23). 47-51.

62. Horbachenko, S. (2020). Cybersecurity as a component of economic security of Ukraine. Galic'kij ekonomičnij visnik. 66. 180-186. 10.33108/galicianvisnyk_tntu2020.05.180.

63. Hoschek, M. (2021). Quantum security and 6G critical infrastructure. Serbian Journal of Engineering Management. 6. 1-8. 10.5937/SJEM2101001H.

64. Hrabchuk, I.L. (2018). Orhanizatsiia zakhystu oblikovoi informatsii v umovakh hibrydnoi viiny [Organization of protection of accounting information in a hybrid war]. Problemy teorii ta metodolohii bukhhalterskoho obliku, kontroliu i analizu – Problems of theory and methodology of accounting, control and analysis. 3 (41). 20-24. DOI: 10.26642/pbo-2018-3(41)-20-24.

65. Huang, R. & Turner, G. (2020). How the UK Can Lead in 5G and 6G Security and Standards. RUSI Newsbrief. Emerging Technologies. 40(7). 10.7945/18ch-1a56.

66. Internet of things (IoT) security threats and concerns worldwide. Statista. URL: https://www.statista.com/statistics/1202640/internet-of-things-security-concerns/

67. Internet Security Threat Report (2019). Symantec. Mountain View: Symantec Corporation. 61 p.

68. Is cybersecurity about more than protection? (2019). EY Global Information Security Survey 2018–19. URL: https://assets.ey.com/content/dam/ey-sites/ey-com/en_gl/topics/advisory/ey-global-information-security-survey-2018-19.pdf?download.

69. Janvrin, Diane & Wang, Tawei (2019). Implications of Cybersecurity on Accounting Information. Journal of Information Systems. Vol. 33. No. 3. A1-A2. DOI: 10.2308/isys-10715.

70. Kafka, Sofiia. (2017). The stages of accounting policies formation. The actual problems of regional economy development. 1. 156-164. 10.15330/apred.1.13.156-164.

71. Karajovic, M., Kim, H.M., Laskowski, M. (2019). Thinking outside the block: projected phases of Blockchain integration in the accounting industry, Australian Accounting Review, Vol. 29 No. 2, 319-330, 10.2139/ssrn.2984126.

72. Kaur, Gurdip, Lashkari, Ziba & Habibi Lashkari, Arash. (2021). Introduction to Cybersecurity. Understanding Cybersecurity Management in FinTech. 17-34. 10.1007/978-3-030-79915-1_2.

73. Khan, A., UL Hassan, Naveed, Y., Zhao, J., Niyato, D., Zhang, Y. & Poor, H. V. (2021). Blockchain and 6G: The Future of Secure and Ubiquitous Communication. ArXiv abs/2106.05673. https://www.researchgate.net/publication/352308474_Blockchain_and_6G_The_Future_of_Secure_and_Ubiquitous_Communication.

74. Kim, Jihyun. (2021). Accountability Policy 2.0: A New Direction of Accountability Policies Based on Every Student Succeeds Act in the U.S. The Korean Educational Administration Society. 39. 69-94. 10.22553/keas.2021.39.2.69.

75. Kohnke, Anne, Shoemaker, Dan. (2015). Making Cybersecurity Effective: The Five Governing Principles for Implementing Practical IT

Governance and Control. EDPACS. 52. 9-17. 10.1080/07366981.2015.1087799.

76. Kokina, J., Mancha, R., Pachamanova, D. (2017). Blockchain: emergent industry adoption and implications for accounting, Journal of Emerging Technologies in Accounting, Vol. 14 No. 2, 91-100, 10.2308/jeta-51911.

77. Kozlowski, S. (2018). An audit ecosystem to support Blockchain-based accounting and assurance book continuous auditing: theory and application, Continuous Auditing: Theory and Application (Rutgers Studies in Accounting Analytics), Emerald Publishing, Bingley, 299-313, 10.1108/978-1-78743-413-420181015.

78. Kumar, Gautam, Singh, Om Prakash & Saini, Hemraj. (2021). Cybersecurity: Ambient Technologies, IoT, and Industry 4.0 Implications. 10.1201/9781003145042.

79. Kuo, Jong-Yih, Liu, Chien-Hung & Lin, Hui-Chi. (2021). Building Graduate Salary Grading Prediction Model Based on Deep Learning. Intelligent Automation & Soft Computing, 27, 53-68. doi: 10.32604/iasc.2021.014437.

80. Kuzlu, Murat, Fair, Corinne & Güler, Özgür. (2021). Role of Artificial Intelligence in the Internet of Things (IoT) cybersecurity. Discover Internet of Things. 1. 10.1007/s43926-020-00001-4.

81. Kyrylieva, L.O. , Postavnyi, A.O. (2010). Orhanizatsiini aspekty obliku nou-khau ta komertsiinoi taiemnytsi v innovatsiinii systemi pidpryiemstva [Organizational aspects of accounting for know-how and trade secrets in the innovation system of the enterprise]. Ekonomichna stratehiia i perspektyvy rozvytku sfery torhivli ta posluh – Economic strategy and prospects for trade and services. 2. 123-130.

82. Lahovska, Olena & Loskorikh, Gabriella. (2020). Formation of Accounting Policy in IT Enterprises. Modern Economics. 19. 108-113. 10.31521/modecon.V19(2020)-18.

83. Lee Gyung Min, Shim ShinWoo, Cho Byoung Mo, Kim TaeKyu & Kim Kyounggon. (2020). The Classification Model of Fileless Cyber Attacks. Journal of KIISE. 47. 454-465. 10.5626/JOK.2020.47.5.454.

84. Lehenchuk, S. F., Tsaruk, I. M., & Nazarenko, T. P. (2021). Pryntsypy zakhystu danykh u systemi obliku: upravlinski aspekty [Principles of data protection in the accounting system: management aspects]. Ekonomika, upravlinnia ta administruvannia – Economics, management and administration, 2(96), 61–69. https://doi.org/10.26642/ema-2021-2(96)-61-69.

85. Lehenchuk, S. F., Horodysky, M. P.; Maistrenko, N. M. (2021). Protection of Accounting Data in the Conditions of Using Internet of Things: Problems and Prospects of Accounting Digitalization. Oblik i Finansi. 91. 12-19. DOI:10.33146/2307-9878-2021-1(91)-12-19.

86. Li, B., Ponson, G., Ezzahi, Y. (2020). Biometrics Security. doi: 10.13140/RG.2.2.26699.41766.

87. Liakhovych, G., Bezruchuk, S., Ivanenko, V. & Laichuk, S. (2019). SWOT-Analysis Of Accounting Outsourcing. European Cooperation. 3. 7-19. 10.32070/ec.v3i43.50.

88. Liu, M., Wu, K., Xu, J. (2019). How will Blockchain technology impact auditing and accounting: permissionless vs. permissioned Blockchain, Current Issues in Auditing, Vol. 13 No. 2, 19-29, 10.2308/ciia-52540.

89. Liu, Z., Wu, L., Ke, J., Qu, W., Wang, W. & Wang, H. (2019). Accountable Outsourcing Location-Based Services With Privacy Preservation. IEEE Access. PP. 1-1. 10.1109/ACCESS.2019.2936582.

90. Loboda, N., Chabaniuk, O. & Senyshyn, B. (2020). Outsourcing as a Mechanism for Accounting Innovations at Ukrainian Enterprises. Business Inform. 2. 329-336. 10.32983/2222-4459-2020-2-329-336.

91. Lu, Yang. (2020). Security in 6G: The Prospects and the Relevant Technologies. Journal of Industrial Integration and Management. 5. 271-289. 10.1142/S2424862220500165.

92. Main incidents in the EU and worldwide. ENISA Threat Landscape. (2020). URL: https://www.enisa.europa.eu/topics/threat-risk-management/threats-and-trends/etl-review-folder/etl-2020-main-incidents.

93. Marasigan, R. (2019). The Role of Ideas that shape the Institutional Change in Cybersecurity: Economic barriers of cyber-attacks. Policy in a Changing World Tackling Global Issues At: Roppongi, Tokyo Japan. 10.6084/m9.figshare.12086763.

94. Marchuk, U. (2012). Komertsiina taiemnytsia: pravova rehlamentatsiia, vidpovidalnist i zakhody shchodo yii zberezhennia [Trade secret: legal regulations, responsibilities and measures to preserve it]. Bukhhalterskyi oblik i audyt – Accounting and auditing. № 5. 49-54.

95. Martyniuk, T. (2016). The Informative Function of Accounting in Outsourcing of the Financial and Accounting Services. Zeszyty Naukowe Uniwersytetu Szczecińskiego Finanse Rynki Finansowe Ubezpieczenia. 2. 151-157. 10.18276/frfu.2016.2.80/2-16.

96. Maszczak, T. (2019). Accounting Outsourcing In Micro And Small Entities – Opportunities And Threats. Prace Naukowe Uniwersytetu Ekonomicznego we Wrocławiu. 63. 92-107. 10.15611/pn.2019.8.07.

97. Mercado-Velazquez, Andres, Escamilla-Ambrosio, P. Jorge & Ortiz-Rodriguez, Floriberto. (2021). A Moving Target Defense Strategy for Internet of Things Cybersecurity. IEEE Access. PP. 1-1. 10.1109/ACCESS.2021.3107403.

98. Milian, K.V., Hrytsiuk, Yu.I. (2013). Osoblyvosti orhanizatsii informatsiinoi bezpeky korporatyvnoi merezhi promyslovoi kompanii [Features of the organization of information security of the corporate network of an industrial company]. Naukovyi visnyk NLTU Ukrainy - Scientific Bulletin of NLTU of Ukraine, 23(4), 314-328.

99. Mobile broadband subscriptions worldwide 2007-2020. Statista. https://www.statista.com/statistics/273016/number-of-mobile-broadband-subscriptions-worldwide-since-2007/

100. Mobile technology share by generation 2016-2025. Statista. https://www.statista.com/statistics/740442/worldwide-share-of-mobile-telecommunication-technology/

101. Moroz, Yu. Yu. & Tsal-Tsalko, Yu.S. (2017). Oblikova polityka pidpryiemstva ta yii kiberbezpeka [Accounting policy of the enterprise and its cybersecurity]. Oblik, analiz i kontrol v umovakh suchasnykh kontseptsii upravlinnia ekonomichnym potentsialom i rynkovoiu vartistiu pidpryiemstva – Accounting, analysis and control in the conditions of modern concepts of management of economic potential and market value of the enterprise. Vol IV. Part I. 8-11.

102. Muravskyi, V., Muravskyi, V., & Shevchuk, O. (2021). Classification of stakeholders (users) of accounting information for the enterprise cybersecurity purposes. Herald of Economics, 1(99), 83-96. doi:https://doi.org/10.35774/visnyk2021.01.083

103. Muravskyi, V., Pochynok, N., & Farion, V. (2021). Classification of cyber risks in accounting. Herald of Economics, 2, 129-144. doi:https://doi.org/10.35774/visnyk2021.02.129.

104. Muravskyi, V.V. (2017). Vplyv hlobalnykh tekhnolohichnykh tendentsii na orhanizatsiiu obliku [The impact of global technological trends on the organization of accounting]. Visnyk Ternopilskoho natsionalnoho ekonomichnoho universytetu – Herald of Ternopil National Economic University. № 4. 138–148. 10.35774/visnyk2017.04.138.

105. Mustafa, Nasir. (2020). Cyber Risk and Covid-19: Managing Cyber Risks Arising From The Pandemic. Brighttalk Webinar Series. Project: Coronavirus CoV-19 to CoV-20 Pro. 10.13140/RG.2.2.12218.82886.

106. Nassimbeni, G., Sartor, M. & Dus, D. (2012). Security risks in service offshoring and outsourcing. Industrial Management and Data Systems. 112. 10.1108/02635571211210059.

107. Nazarenko, O. & Surovitskaya, A. (2018). Accounting outsourcing: advantages, disadvantages, and peculiarities of introduction. Ekonomika ta derzhava. 50. 10.32702/2306-6806.2018.12.50.

108. Neil, G. (2012). Accounting for Employee Benefits. Counting the Poor: New Thinking About European Poverty Measures and Lessons for the United States. doi: 10.1093/acprof:oso/9780199860586.003.0007.

109. Nekhai, V. A., Nekhai, V. V. (2017). Informatsiina bezpeka yak skladova ekonomichnoi bezpeky pidpryiemstv [Information security as a component of economic security of enterprises]. Naukovyi visnyk Mizhnarodnoho humanitarnoho universytetu – Scientific Bulletin of the International Humanities University. 24(2). 137-140.

110. Nicholson, B. & Aman, A. (2012). Managing attrition in offshore finance and accounting outsourcing: Exploring the interplay of competing institutional logics. Strategic Outsourcing: An International Journal. 5. 10.1108/17538291211291765.

111. Number of Blockchain wallet users worldwide. Statista. https://www.statista.com/statistics/647374/worldwide-blockchain-wallet-users/

112. Number of cryptocurrencies worldwide from 2013 to 2021. Statista. https://www.statista.com/statistics/863917/number-crypto-coins-tokens/

113. O'Leary, D.E. (2017). Configuring blockchain architectures for transaction information in blockchain consortiums: the case of accounting and supply chain systems, Intelligent Systems in Accounting, Finance and Management, Vol. 24 No. 4, 138-147, doi: 10.1002/isaf.1417.

114. Ocheretko, L. & Udovychenko, H. (2020). Improvement of Salary Accounting at the Enterprise. Efektyvna ekonomika, 12. doi: 10.32702/2307-2105-2020.12.101.

115. Patterson, W. & Gergely, M. (2020). Economic Prospect Theory Applied to Cybersecurity. Advances in Human Factors in Cybersecurity. 113-121. 10.1007/978-3-030-52581-1_15.

116. Pendley, John. (2018). Finance and Accounting Professionals and Cybersecurity Awareness. Journal of Corporate Accounting & Finance. 29. 53-58. DOI: 10.1002/jcaf.22291.

117. Perevalova, L.V., Kvasha, S.V. (2011) Zakhyst konfidentsiinoi informatsii: problemy ta shliakhy vyrishennia [Protection of confidential information: problems and solutions]. Visnyk Natsionalnoho tekhnichnoho universytetu «Kharkivskyi politekhnichnyi instytut»: Tematychnyi vypusk: Aktualni problemy rozvytku ukrainskoho suspilstva – Visnyk Natsionalnoho tekhnichnoho universytetu «Kharkivskyi politekhnichnyi instytut»: Tematychnyi vypusk: Aktualni problemy rozvytku ukrainskoho suspilstva. № 30. 179 p.

118. Petruk, O. M., Novak, O. S. (2017). Sutnist kryptovaliuty yak metodolohichna peredumova yii oblikovoho vidobrazhennia [The essence of cryptocurrency as a methodological prerequisite for its accounting]. Visnyk ZhDTU – Bulletin of ZhSTU, 4 (82). 48-55.

119. Pidsumky 2018 roku v tsyfrakh [Results of 2018 in figures]. URL: https://cyberpolice.gov.ua/results/2018.

120. Pimentel, E., Bouliann, E. (2020). Blockchain in Accounting Research and Practice: Current Trends and Future Opportunities. Accounting Perspectives. 19 (3). 325–361. 19. 10.1111/1911-3838.12239.

121. Popivniak, Yu. M. (2019). Kiberbezpeka ta zakhyst bukhhalterskykh danykh v umovakh zastosuvannia novitnikh informatsiinykh tekhnolohii [Cybersecurity and protection of accounting data in the application of the latest information technologies]. Biznes

Inform – Business Inform. 8. 150–157. DOI: 10.32983/2222-4459-2019-8-150-157.

122. Popovski, P., Chiariotti, F., Huang, K., Kalør, A., Kountouris, M., Pappas, N. & Soret, B. (2021). A Perspective on Time towards Wireless 6G.

123. Porambage, P., Gür, G., Osorio, D. P. M., Liyanage, M., Gurtov, A. & Ylianttila, M. (2021).The Roadmap to 6G Security and Privacy. IEEE Open Journal of the Communications Society, vol. 2,1094-1122. 10.1109/OJCOMS.2021.3078081.

124. Prakash, Febin, Baskar, Kala & Sadawarti, Harsh. (2019). Cyber Crime: Challenges and its Classification. International Multi-disciplinary Academic Research Conference (IMARC-2019). 2–4.

125. Pro osnovni zasady zabezpechennia kiberbezpeky Ukrainy. (2017). Zakon Ukrainy [Law of Ukraine "On Basic Principles of Cybersecurity of Ukraine"]. October 5, 2017. № 2163-VIII. URL: http://zakon3.rada.gov.ua/laws/show/2163-19.

126. Pushkar M.S., Shchyrba M.T. (2010). Teoriia i praktyka formuvannia oblikovoi polityky : monohrafiia [Theory and practice of accounting policy: a monograph.]. Ternopil : Kart-blansh, 2010. 260 p.

127. Pylypenko, A. (2019). Outsourcing of Accounting Services: Consideration of Contractual Aspects. Scientific Bulletin of the National Academy of Statistics, Accounting and Audit. 30-39. 10.31767/nasoa.3.2019.03.

128. Radchenko, M. A. (2015). Osoblyvosti vidobrazhennia elektronnykh hroshei v obliku [Features of the reflection of electronic money in accounting]. Naukovyi visnyk Uzhhorodskoho universytetu. Seriia : Ekonomika – Scientific Bulletin of Uzhgorod National University. Series: Economics, Issue 1(2). 121-124.

129. Rajput, B. (2020). Exploring the Phenomenon of Cyber Economic Crime. Cyber Economic Crime in India. 53-78. 10.1007/978-3-030-44655-0_4.

130. Rasche, A. & Esser, D. (2006). From Stakeholder Management to Stakeholder Accountability. Journal of Business Ethics. 65. 251-267. 10.1007/s10551-005-5355-y.

131. Revenok V.I., Mamchur O.S. Osnovni aspekty informatsiinykh system z obliku narakhuvannia zarobitnoi platy [The main aspects of information systems for payroll accounting]. Molodyi vchenyi – A young scientist. 2015. № 2 (17). 22-25.

132. Rındasu, S.M. (2019). Blockchain in accounting: trick or treat?, Quality Access to Success, Vol. 20 No. 170, 143-147.

133. Risk committees. The Institute of Chartered Accountants in England and Wales. Retrived from: https://www.icaew.com/technical/corporate-governance/committees/risk-committees.

134. Rodrigues, B., Franco, M., Parangi, G. & Stiller, B. (2019). SEConomy: A Framework for the Economic Assessment of Cybersecurity. Economics of Grids, Clouds, Systems, and Services, 16th International Conference, GECON 2019, Leeds, UK, September 17–19, 2019. 154-166. 10.1007/978-3-030-36027-6_13.

135. Rohan, Rohani, Funilkul, Suree, Pal, Debajyoti & Thapliyal, Himanshu. (2021). Humans in the Loop: Cybersecurity Aspects in the Consumer IoT Context. IEEE Consumer Electronics Magazine. 99. 1-10. 10.1109/MCE.2021.3095385.

136. Rosenzweig, Paul. (2011). 10 Conservative Principles for Cybersecurity Policy. The Heritage Foundation for Leadership of America. 2513. URL: http://thf_media.s3.amazonaws.com/2011/pdf/bg2513.pdf.

137. Rozheliuk, V.M. (2013). Zakhody zabezpechennia zakhystu oblikovoi informatsii [Measures to ensure the protection of accounting

information]. Bukhhalterskyi oblik, analiz ta audyt: problemy teorii, metodolohii, orhanizatsii – Accounting, analysis and audit: problems of theory, methodology, organization. 2 (12). 335–340.

138. Rue, R., Pfleeger, S. (2009). Making the Best Use of Cybersecurity Economic Models. Security & Privacy, IEEE. 7. 52 - 60. 10.1109/MSP.2009.98.

139. Sakharov, P.O. (2017). Okremi aspekty obliku elektronnykh hroshei ta osoblyvosti provedennia yikh analizu ta audytu u bankakh [Some aspects of electronic money accounting and features of their analysis and audit in banks]. Mukachivskyi derzhavnyi universytet – Mukachevo state university, 9. 1192-1197.

140. Samudrage, D. & Jayewardene, D. (2019). Post-Implementation Benefits and Challenges of the Balanced Scorecard: Evidence from the Finance and Accounting Outsourcing Sector. 10. 86-99. 10.7176/RJFA/10-22-10.

141. Sarkar, S. (2018). Blockchain accounting the disruption ahead, The Management Accountant Journal, Vol. 6, 73-78.

142. Saydjari, O. (2019). Engineering trustworthy systems: A principled approach to cybersecurity. Communications of the ACM. 62. 63-69. 10.1145/3282487.

143. Schaffner, Georg, Grove, Laura, Holder, Anthony Hugh & Mac, Clouse. (2018). Cybersecurity Guidance for Accountants and Executives. Internal Auditing, Vol. 33, No. 5, 5-20.

144. Schmitt, Michael. (2012). Classification of Cyber Conflict. Journal of Conflict and Security Law. 17 (2). 245-260. 10.1093/jcsl/krs018.

145. Schmitz, J., Leoni, G. (2019). Accounting and auditing at the time of Blockchain technology: a research agenda, The Management Accountant Journal, Vol. 29 No. 2, 331-342, doi: 10.1111/auar.12286.

146. Sectoral thematic threat analysis ETL2020. (2020). ENISA Threat Landscape. European Union Agency for Cybersecurity. URL :

https://www.enisa.europa.eu/publications/sectoral-thematic-threat-analysis/at_download/fullReport. doi: 10.2824/552242.

147. Semenyshena, N., Khorunzhak, N. & Sadovska, I. Evaluation of the Adaptability of the Scientific Theories for the Development of Accounting Institute. Intellectual Economics. 2020. 14(1). P.114-129. 10.13165/IE-2014-1-07.

148. Semenyshena, N., Sysiuk, S., Shevchuk, K., Petruk, I., Benko, I. (2020). Institutionalism in Accounting: a Requirement of the Times or a Mechanism of Social Pressure? Independent Journal of Management & Production, 11(9), 2516-2541. doi: http://dx.doi.org/10.14807/ijmp.v11i9.1440.

149. Seo, Jinsil, Bruner, Michael, Payne, Austin, Gober, Nathan, McMullen, Donald & Chakravorty, Dhruva. (2019). Using Virtual Reality to Enforce Principles of Cybersecurity. The Journal of Computational Science Education. 10. 81-87. 10.22369/issn.2153-4136/10/1/13.

150. Shchyrska, A. Yu. (2018). Vymohy korystuvachiv do yakosti oblikovoi informatsii [User requirements for the quality of accounting information]. Ekonomichnyi prostir. – Economic space. № 139. 213-228.

151. Sheehan, Barry, Murphy, Finbarr, Kia, Arash & Kiely, Ronan. (2021). A quantitative bow-tie cyber risk classification and assessment framework. Journal of Risk Research. 1-20. 10.1080/13669877.2021.1900337.

152. Sheldon, M.D. (2018). Using Blockchain to aggregate and share misconduct issues across the accounting profession, Current Issues in Auditing, Vol. 12 No. 2, 27-35, doi: 10.2308/ciia-52184.

153. Shevchuk, O., Desyatnyuk, O., Voitseshyn, V., Bryk, M. & Muravskyi, V. (2020). Control and Accounting of the Transportation Services Self-cost using GPS. 631-634. 10.1109/ACIT49673.2020.9208973.

154. Shitova, Yu. & Shitov, Y. (2019). Contemporary Trends in Economic Cybersecurity. The world of new economy. 13. 22-30. 10.26794/2220-6469-2019-13-4-22-30.

155. Shpak, V.A. (2015). Orhanizatsiia zakhystu oblikovoi informatsii [Organization of protection of accounting information]. Bukhhalterskyi oblik, analiz ta audyt: problemy teorii, metodolohii, orhanizatsii – Accounting, analysis and audit: problems of theory, methodology, organization. 2. 181–187.

156. Shyshkova, N. L. (2016). Zasoby pidvyshchennia kerovanosti bezpekoiu oblikovoi informatsii [Means to improve the security of accounting information]. Ekonomichnyi visnyk Natsionalnoho hirnychoho universytetu – Economic Journal of the National Mining University. № 3. 119-127. URL: http://nbuv.gov.ua/UJRN/evngu_2016_3_17.

157. Šikanjić, Nedeljko, Avramović, Zoran & Marinković, Dražen. (2021). Cybersecurity IoT Architecture: One Proposed Solution for the Security Risks and Threats. The 1st International Conference on Maritime Education and Development. pp.325-331. 10.1007/978-3-030-64088-0_29.

158. Sinha, S. (2020). Blockchain – opportunities and challenges for accounting professionals, Journal of Corporate Accounting and Finance, Vol. 31, 65-67, 10.1002/jcaf.22430.

159. Sinno, S. & Hawley, C. (2020). How biometrics can save companies from 'fire and forget'. Biometric Technology Today, 7, 5-8. doi: 10.1016/S0969-4765(20)30095-3.

160. Siriwardhana, Y., Porambage, P., Liyanage, M. & Ylianttila, M. (2021). AI and 6G Security: Opportunities and Challenges. Joint European Conference on Networks and Communications (EuCNC) & 6G Summit. Porto, Portugal. https://www.researchgate.net/publication/350824466_AI_and_6G_Security_Opportunities_and_Challenges

161. Size of the Internet of Things (IoT) security market worldwide from 2016 to 2025. Statista. URL: https://www.statista.com/statistics/993789/worldwide-internet-of-things-security-market-size/

162. Smith, E. (2020). How will IoT benefit the accounting profession? Retrieved from https://www.itproportal.com/features/how-will-iotbenefit-the-accounting-profession.

163. Smith, Kane, Dhillon, Gurpreet & Carter, Lemuria. (2021). User values and the development of a cybersecurity public policy for the IoT. International Journal of Information Management. 56. 10.1016/j.ijinfomgt.2020.102123.

164. Sofiah, Aman, A., Maelah, R., Amiruddin, R. & Hamzah, N. (2013). Management control in accounting outsourcing services. Business Strategy Series. 14. 43-49. 10.1108/17515631311325097.

165. Spitters, Thomas & Heaton, CPA (2019). A Supplement to Cybersecurity Breviary for Accountants Kindle Edition. Baume Verlag, San Francisco. 61 p.

166. Steingartner, William & Galinec, Darko. (2021). Cyber Threats and Cyber Deception in Hybrid Warfare. Acta Polytechnica Hungarica. 18. 25-45. 10.12700/APH.18.3.2021.3.2.

167. Stitilis, D., Rotomskis, I., Laurinaitis, M., Nadvynychnyy, S., Khorunzhak, N. (2020). National Cybersecurity Strategies: Management, Unification and Assessment. Independent Journal of Management & Production. 11 (9). 2341-2354. 10.14807/ijmp.v11i9.1431.

168. Strupczewski, Grzegorz. (2021). Defining cyber risk. Safety Science. 6. 135. 10.1016/j.ssci.2020.105143.

169. Summary Report / Telstra Security Report 2019 (2019). Paddington : Telstra Corporation Limited. 19 p.

170. Sun, Zhenjun, Li, Qi, Liu, Yunfan & Zhu, Yuhao. (2021). Opportunities and Challenges for Biometrics. China's e-Science Blue Book 2020, 101-125. doi: 10.1007/978-981-15-8342-1_6.

171. Syrotiuk, O. (2010). Pravo na komertsiinu taiemnytsiu [The right to trade secrets]. Balans – Balance. № 95. 57–59.

172. Systema obliku robochoho chasu «STOP-Time 4.0» [Working time accounting system "STOP-Time 4.0"]. (2016). K.:TOV «Kard-Sistems». 62 p.

173. Tan, B.S., Low, K.Y. (2019). Blockchain as the database engine in the accounting system, Australian Accounting Review, Vol. 29 No. 2, 312-318, 10.1111/auar.12278.

174. The 2019 Kearney Global Services Location Index. (2020). Digital resonance: the new factor influencing location attractiveness. URL: https://www.kearney.com/digital-transformation/gsli/2019-full-report.

175. Tiron Tudor, A., Deliu, D., Farcane, N., Donțu, A. (2021). Managing change with and through blockchain in accountancy organizations: a systematic literature review. Journal of Organizational Change Management. ahead-of-print. 10.1108/JOCM-10-2020-0302.

176. Tsimperidis, Ioannis, Yucel, Cagatay, Katos, Vasilios. (2021). Age and Gender as Cyber Attribution Features in Keystroke Dynamic-Based User Classification Processes. Electronics. 10. 835. 10.3390/electronics10070835.

177. Value of cryptocurrency theft worldwide from 2016 to 2020. Statista. https://www.statista.com/statistics/960226/theft-of-cryptocurrency-value/

178. Viter, S. A., Svitlyshyn, I. I. (2017). Zakhyst oblikovoi informatsii ta kiberbezpeka pidpryiemstva [Protection of accounting information and cybersecurity of the enterprise]. Ekonomika ta suspilstvo : elektronne naukove fakhove vydannia – Economy and society: electronic scientific professional publication. 11. 497–502.

179. Volosovych, S., Klapkiv, L. (2018). Determinanty vynyknennia ta realizatsii kiberryzykiv [Determinants of the origin and implementation of cyber risks]. Zovnishnia torhivlia: ekonomika, finansy, pravo – Foreign trade: economics, finance, law. 3. 101–115. URL: http://nbuv.gov.ua/UJRN/uazt_2018_3_10.

180. Wang, M., Zhu, T., Zhang, T., Zhang, J., Yu, S. & Zhou, W. (2020). Security and privacy in 6G networks: New areas and new challenges. Digital Communications and Networks. 6. 10.1016/j.dcan.2020.07.003.

181. Wilson, K., Hugh J. (2014). Cybersecurity Economics: How Much Cybersecurity is Enough?. Australian intellectual property journal. 7-9.

182. World Digital Competitiveness Ranking IMD 2018. https://www.imd.org/wcc/world-competitiveness-center-rankings/world-digital-competitiveness-rankings-2018.

183. Worldwide spending on blockchain solutions from 2017 to 2025. Statista. https://www.statista.com/statistics/800426/worldwide-blockchain-solutions-spending/

184. Wu, J., Xiong, F., Li, C. (2019). Application of internet of Things and blockchain technologies toimprove accounting, IEEE Access, Vol. 20, 1-10, 10.1109/ACCESS.2019.2930637.

185. Yak pysaty i vymovliaty bitcoin [How to write and pronounce bitcoin]. (2021). Available at https://www.bbc.com/ukrainian/blog-olexandr-ponomariv-41225133.

186. Yanchev, A.V. (2015). Elektronnyi oblik pratsi ta yii oplaty – osnova derzhavnoi stratehii formuvannia liudskoho kapitalu [Electronic accounting of labor and its payment is the basis of the state strategy of human capital formation]. Visny`k XNAU im. V.V. Dokuchayeva – Bulletin of KNAU named after V.V. Dokuchaev, 2. 212-221.

187. Yatsyk, T.V. (2017). Metodyka finansovoho obliku kryptovaliuty yak osoblyvoho vydu elektronnykh hroshei [Methods of financial accounting of cryptocurrency as a special type of electronic money]. Molodyi vchenyi – Young scientist, 2 (42). 349–354.

188. Yevdokymov, V.V. (2011). Nadiinist bukhhalterskoi informatsii yak peredumova zabezpechennia ekonomichnoi bezpeky pidpryiemstva [Reliability of accounting information as a prerequisite for ensuring the economic security of the enterprise]. Visnyk ZhDTU – Herald of ZhSTU. 3 (57). 46-50.

189. Ylianttila, M., Kantola, R., Gurtov, A., Mucchi, L., & Oppermann I., (Eds.). (2020). 6G White Paper: Research Challenges For Trust, Security And Privacy [White paper]. (6G Research Visions, No. 9). University of Oulu. http://urn.fi/urn:isbn:9789526226804.

190. Zadorozhny, Z., Muravskyi, V. V., Shevchuk, O. A., Sudyn, Y. A. (2018). Management accounting of the settlements with contractors in innovative environment of business communications. Marketing and Management of Innovations, 2, 103-112. 10.21272/mmi.2018.2-09.

191. Zadorozhnyi, Z. -M., Muravskyi, V. and Muravskyi, V. (2021). Combined Outsourcing of Accounting and Cybersecurity Authorities, 11th International Conference on Advanced Computer Information Technologies (ACIT). 544-547. https://doi.org/10.1109/ACIT52158.2021.9548649.

192. Zadorozhnyi, Z. -M., Muravskyi, V. and Shevchuk, O. (2021). Influence of Organizational Factors and Forms of Accounting Outsourcing on Enterprise Cybersecurity. 11th International Conference on Advanced Computer Information Technologies (ACIT). 540-543. https://doi.org/10.1109/ACIT52158.2021.9548370.

193. Zadorozhnyi, Z.-M., Muravskyi, V. (2020) Analysis of the implementation efficiency of the new computer-communication form of accounting. ACIT'2020: 10th International Conference on Advanced

Computer Information Technologies. Deggendorf, Germany, September 16-18. 718-721. https://doi.org/10.1109/ACIT49673.2020.9208973.

194. Zadorozhnyi, Z. V., Muravskyi, V. V., Sudyn, Yu. A. Goodwill assessment in enterprise management: innovative approaches using computer and communication technologies. Marketing and management of innovation. 2018. 4. 43-53. http://doi.org/10.21272/mmi.2018.4-04.

195. Zadorozhnyi, Z., Muravskyi, V., & Shevchuk, O. (2018) Management accounting of electronic transactions with the use of cryptocurrencies. Financial And Credit Activity: Problems Of Theory And Practice, 3(26), 169-177. doi: 10.18371/fcaptp.v3i26.144368

196. Zadorozhnyi, Z., Muravskyi, V., Shevchuk, O. & Muravskyi, V. (2020). The accounting system as the basis for organising enterprise cybersecurity. Financial and credit activity: problems of theory and practice. 3. 147-156. 10.18371/fcaptp.v3i34.215462.

197. Zadorozhnyi, Z.-M., Muravskyi, V., Pochynok, N., & Hrytsyshyn, A. (2020). Innovation Management and Automated Accounting in the Chaotic Storage Logistics. Marketing and Management of Innovations, 2, 313-323. http://doi.org/10.21272/mmi.2020.2-23.

198. Zadorozhnyi, Z.-M., Ometsinska, I., & Muravskiy, V. (2021). Determinants of Firm's Innovation: Increasing the Transparency of Financial Statements. Marketing and Management of Innovations, 2, 74-86. http://doi.org/10.21272/mmi.2021.2-06.

199. Zadorozhnyy, Z.-M., Muravskiy, V., Yatsyshyn, S., & Shevchuk, O. (2021). Accounting of wages with the use of biometrics to ensure cybersecurity of enterprises. Financial and Credit Activity: Problems of Theory and Practice, 3(38), 162–172. https://doi.org/10.18371/fcaptp.v3i38.237446.

200. Zhang, J., Wang, Z., Wang, D., Zhang, X., Gupta, B B., Liu, X. & Ma, J. (2021). A Secure Decentralized Spatial Crowdsourcing Scheme

for 6G-Enabled Network in Box. IEEE Transactions on Industrial Informatics. 1-11. 10.1109/TII.2021.3081416.

201. Zinkevich, V., Shtatov, D. (2007). Informacionnye riski: analiz i kolichestvennaja ocenk [Information risks: analysis and quantitative assessment]. Buhgalterija i banki – Accounting and banks. 1. 50–55 [In Russian].

202. Zoidze, D. R. (2017). The Outsourcing and Peculiarities of Its Application in the Pharmaceutical Industry Sector. Business Inform. 5, 274–278.

SCIENTIFIC PUBLICATION

Volodymyr Muravskyi

ACCOUNTING AND CYBERSECURITY

Monograph

Format 60x84 1/16. Times New Roman
Offset paper. Duplicator printing.
Order № 0178-2021
Circulation 100 p,

Kindle Publishing,
Box 81226 Seattle,
WA 98108-1226,
USA
2021